Rosemary Bidwell, a daughter of a Baptist Minister, was born in Somerset. A former nurse, college lecturer and bridal designer, she owned her highly successful bridal business 'Exclusive by Design' in Warwick where she became the first woman Rotarian. It was through her work with Rotary International, she went out to Sierra Leone in 2003 to see the devastation caused by the civil war. This was to change her life. She took a step of faith, sold her business and set up her own charity devoting the rest of her life to caring for orphaned and abandoned street children in Sierra Leone, West Africa.

This book is dedicated to my wonderful children in Sierra Leone.

They are Augustine who is the eldest, Momoh, Hassan, Mohammed, Ibrahim and little Alimamy.

And the girls are Alimatu, Ishiatu, Nancy, N'Mah, Aminata, Haja, Fatmata, Bintu, Saffie Conteh and Saffie Kanga and last but not least Rosie.

It is also dedicated to the Rev Dennis Bidwell and Mrs Bidwell, who were my parents. Without them, I may not have known the true meaning of caring for others.

Rosemary Bidwell

A STORY OF HOPE AND HAPPINESS

SEEING LIFE THROUGH AFRICAN EYES

AUSTIN MACAULEY PUBLISHERS™

LONDON • CAMBRIDGE • NEW YORK • SHARJAH

A CIP catalogue record for this title is available from the British Library.

ISBN 9781398433113 (Paperback)
ISBN 9781398433120 (Hardback)
ISBN 9781398433137 (ePub e-book)

www.austinmacauley.com

First Published 2023
Austin Macauley Publishers Ltd®
1 Canada Square
Canary Wharf
London
E14 5AA

I would like to thank all those who have been part of my journey in the life of The Cotton Tree Children's Trust.

To those who I have taken out to Sierra Leone, whose lives have been greatly enriched.

To all the fundraisers, who gave up their valuable time, and all the children who did exceptional things to raise much-needed funds.

To all the committee members, who supported me through good times and bad.

To all the children's wonderful sponsors, without whom, our children would not be where they are today.

And to Ron, my wonderful husband, who has supported me in writing this book and has picked up the pieces of shattered hopes and dreams, and stood by me every step of the way since May 2016 when we met.

Table of Contents

Chapter 1: In the Beginning and Stepping onto African Soil   11

Chapter 2: The Start of a New Life   19

Chapter 3: The Charity Is Born   24

Chapter 4: Finding Our New Home   29

Chapter 5: Things Don't Always Go as Planned   32

Chapter 6: A Holiday Like No Other   35

Chapter 7: 2007 Our First Ten Children   40

Chapter 8: The Opening of Our New Home   49

Chapter 9: Our Second Intake of Children   52

Chapter 10: Life Goes On   63

Chapter 11: On the Move to a Bigger Home   68

Chapter 12: The First Time in Our New Home   74

Chapter 13: Daily Life in Sierra Leone   80

Chapter 14: Fundraising in the UK   93

Chapter 15: Assaulted and Abused   97

Chapter 16: Frustrations Galore!   100

Chapter 17: To Hell and Back   109

Chapter 18: Where to Now?   114

Chapter 19: Starting All Over Again   118

Chapter 20: The Children Are Brainwashed   121

Chapter 21: A Rainbow of Hope   125

Chapter 22: I Have a Dream   130

Appendix: In Their Own Words   133

Chapter 1
In the Beginning and
Stepping onto African Soil

As a child, I was brought up in a Baptist Manse, as my father was a Baptist minister. Every year on Christmas Day, my parents would place a small square box on the dinner table. On the box, it would say, 'think of those less fortunate than yourselves this Christmas' and every year I would go upstairs and get some of my pocket money and place it in the box. Until one year, when I was older, I asked my father more about where our money was going. This really touched my heart, and I ran upstairs and emptied all my pocket money out on my bed. I sat there for a while looking at it, and then I collected up every penny I had and took it downstairs and placed it in the box. My father saw what I had done and said, "When you give all that you have, it really hurts, but that's when you really give from your heart."

I had always wanted to become a nurse from the age of ten, do my midwifery, go out to Africa and work with mothers and babies.

Finally, at the age of eighteen, I left home to do my nursing training at Addenbrooke's Hospital in Cambridge. I absolutely loved it, but I hurt my back and eventually I had to finish.

I had always loved dressmaking as a child and used to cut and alter some of my clothes. I remember my mother made me a pair of blue wool trousers, which were so uncomfortable, so I cut them up and made a skirt!

At the age of eleven, I made my first dress. I went into Cambridge where we had a wonderful fabric shop called Gordon Thodays and chose my dress fabric, which was blue cotton satin with a sort of green cabbage-like flowers on it. I looked for a pattern I liked, bought it, and came home on the 104 bus to Histon where I lived. I opened up the pattern and as it was all in American, I had a job to follow it as it referred to the top as 'the vest' so I decided the best thing to do was to look at the pictures and diagrams and work back from there and somehow I made it! I loved that dress and can still remember wearing it!

I went on from there and at the age of thirteen, made my first wool suit, which was a beautiful turquoise colour, for Easter! This was a bit trickier as it was so thick and I had a job to get it under my mother's old hand Singer sewing machine, but I did it!

When I had to finish nursing, I decided to go and study Fashion and Design and take my dressmaking to a whole new level. My next-door neighbour asked me to make her sister's wedding dress. As I had made mine and my bridesmaids' dresses, I said yes! People began asking me to make their wedding dresses and I absolutely loved it! It seemed to come so naturally. I was selected by the BBC to go on a course up in the Wirral in Cheshire with TV presenter Ann Ladbury, who had a daily show with dressmaking in the 1970s. I couldn't quite believe it! I found myself amongst other women who appeared to be much better than me. There was an exam at the end of the course, and I did very well. This gave me the confidence to go further and start my own business.

I was working from home initially, but it was clear that I needed to take the next step. I became a lecturer and taught further education in colleges and schools. It was time to branch out and get my own premises, so I found a wonderful old, beamed studio in the heart of Warwick where I began designing and making bespoke wedding dresses. My business was called Exclusive by Design and within two years, I had outgrown the studio. I used to look across the market square and see the perfect shop. I imagine my wedding gowns standing in the windows for all to see. As I sat in my studio, I heard that the shop over the road was becoming vacant. This was my chance, and within a few months, it was mine! I had my sign over the shop and took on more staff. I absolutely loved it! I would still be there at eight o'clock some nights when others would come into town smelling of expensive after-shave and perfumes to enjoy their night out.

I was asked to do fashion shows at bridal fayres and even did the fashion shows at the Town and Country show in Warwickshire for six years.

Exclusive By Design by Rosemary   Rosemary pattern drafting

In 2000, I was asked to join Rotary and was the first woman Rotarian in Warwick. It wasn't long before I became chairman of International, where we were supporting projects overseas. One of these was in Sierra Leone, West Africa.

I set about organising a Gala Dinner with Sir Norman Wisdom to raise money for this project. As a child, Norman was abandoned and ran away at the age of fourteen to join the forces. He lied about his age to become accepted, and it wasn't long before he was entertaining the troops with his infectious humour.

Along with my bridal business, I set up a wedding car hire business in which we had a gold Rolls Royce and a white limousine. One of our chauffeurs knew Norman Wisdom and that is how I got to know him. He loved our Rolls Royce and always wanted to sit in the front and play with the windows and knobs and wave to everybody as we went by!

Sir Norman Wisdom with our cars

Norman Wisdom with Rosemary

With the money we raised, which was well over £3,000, I wanted to see for myself where it was going so decided I'd like to take myself out to Sierra Leone to see the project for myself.

I got in touch with the charity head office in Salisbury, Wiltshire to ask more about the project in Sierra Leone. I went down for a meeting to discuss the possibilities. As I drove back home I was in a daze, as the long-awaited dream of finally being given the chance to go out to Africa was becoming a reality.

I set about getting all my vaccinations and felt more like one of the pincushions we used in the shop!

The day finally came. February 22, 2003. I remember standing at the flight information board at Heathrow airport with my heavy haversack on my back, shaking with nervous excitement as I looked up and down for the flight that said 'Freetown, Sierra Leone'.

I had finally done it! I was about to start a completely new chapter in my life and see Africa for the very first time!

The plane was full, and I was the only white person on it! I felt very conspicuous.

As we took off, the African woman passenger beside me got out her Bible and started reading it! I became a little concerned at this point, wondering if she knew something I didn't! I soon settled down and felt quite at home in an odd sort of way. It was clearly an old plane with no mod cons and the only inflight entertainment were the people on it! There was a lot of noise, and everyone seemed to know everyone else.

After the long flight, I was soon to see my first glimpse of Africa. The red dusty ground and the little mud huts. As we landed, everyone let out an almighty big cheer as if it were something of a miracle that we had arrived at all!

As I stepped off the plane and onto the tarmac, I could smell the hot humid air, which was to become my home. The arrivals area, as it was called, was just that. An area with concrete floors and not a lounge, as we know it!

It was totally chaotic. I had never experienced anything like it! Everyone was shouting and it was every man or woman for themselves. I had many offers of help with my bags, but I knew they only wanted to help me because I was white and to them, this only meant one thing – I had money!

I stood my ground and retrieved my bag and found my way outside in pitch darkness to where an old clapped-out bus was waiting to take us down to the river to catch the equally clapped-out ferry. This was shared with goats, chickens, baskets of fish and numerous other things as well as many baskets of fruit! This is where I met the first African children living on the beach. They knew we had just landed so they hung around to see if any of us would give them money.

It took well over an hour to reach the other side. There is no direct airport in Sierra Leone, so you have to fly to Lungi, and then go by ferry to the mainland of Sierra Leone.

I was met by some people from England who were out there working on the same project as I was fundraising for. We all climbed into an old jeep to find the place we were staying. It was called a hotel, but not as we know it!

This was the start of a new life-changing adventure and one that was to change my life.

The hotel (such as it was) was by the sea and in the morning, I caught my first glimpse of Africa.

We were there to work on the project I raised money for, which was homes for orphans and abandoned children, whose parents had either been killed or had fled during the eleven-year bloody civil war.

Nothing could have prepared me for the devastation that greeted me.

Families had been burnt to death in their homes, and people who had been captured by the rebels were torn limb from limb, being given a stark choice, 'short sleeve or long sleeve' – meaning they would chop their hands off for long sleeve or chop their arms off to their elbows for a short sleeve! They would also chop legs off to above the knee to stop them from escaping!

Children were left crying on the streets to survive as best they could or die, and many simply didn't make it.

I saw child mothers aged between twelve and fifteen who had been raped by the rebels and made pregnant, then used as slaves. The rebels and young boys had been drugged and forced to train as boy soldiers to kill.

There was no infrastructure, no sanitation, no electricity, no running water, no animals so no milk, no buses, no postal service…no nothing!

There is a film that was made, called *Blood Diamond*, with Leonardo DiCaprio, and it depicted the atrocities of the civil war in Sierra Leone. Every time I watch it, tears fall down my face as I saw the reality of what actually happened.

A whole family burnt alive in this house

Two men that had their arm and leg cut off by the rebels

What I saw had changed my life forever.

There were mattresses on a concrete floor full of tiny babies who had lost their parents. It was a pitiful sight. They didn't ask to be born and they didn't deserve to die!

A house (above) and Kroo Bay (below) where whole families lived….and died!

Chapter 2
The Start of a New Life

I returned home some six weeks later, a challenged and changed person, traumatised by what I had witnessed. I couldn't get the images out of my head and for eight weeks after I came back, I was transported back to the sights and sounds that I had witnessed as I tried to sleep.

Thanks to my devoted staff at my shop, I returned to Sierra Leone again three months later to see what I could do to help. I was working with child mothers who had been raped by the rebels, ended up pregnant and having babies.

I used to be a foster mother and gave respite foster care to special needs babies and small children when my children were young.

The local newspaper heard of what I was doing and decided to do an article about it. As a result of seeing the article, a paramedic called Simon Greenfield got in touch and asked if he could come out with me next time to help.

At the same time, I had been making a wedding dress for a client, whose sister used to come in with her. She too became interested and wanted to fly out with Simon and me.

They had to have all their injections as I did, and we all set off for another adventure. I had prepared them as much as I could about what they would see, but it didn't compare to the real thing.

We stayed in a 'hotel', and they came to work with me to see the project I was raising money for. I was there to teach much-needed skills, and to educate these young, innocent child mothers.

It was here that I met a young child mother, aged just fourteen, called Abibatu Solomon who was living on the streets and had just given birth to a baby girl she called Mamunatu. She had a friend called Frances who had also just given birth to a baby boy she called Mohammed. Whilst working with them, one day I heard Abi call 'Mum'! She was calling me and had decided she wanted to adopt me as her mum! Both her parents had been killed, and at the age of nine, she fled on the back of a lorry to the capital of Sierra Leone, Freetown, where she slept under the market tables and ate scraps of food to survive.

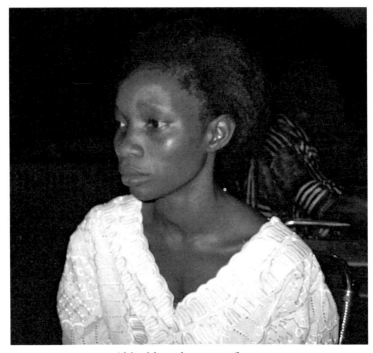
Abi without hope or a future

Abi and Francis with their babies

Whilst working there, we decided to have their babies christened to formally name them. You don't have birth certificates unless you are rich and can afford them! Everything comes down to food and water. What is more important, a birth certificate, or rice in your stomach?

The night before the christening, I heard Abi call, "Mum, I want to change the name of my baby, I want to call her Rosemary after you because you have saved my life."

What a surprise! I wasn't expecting that! I felt very humbled.

In a short space of time, I had gone out to save these poor children from a life of poverty and to give what I had to help them. In return, I gained a daughter and granddaughter to add to my own grown-up family.

Abi (right) and Frances with their babies being christened

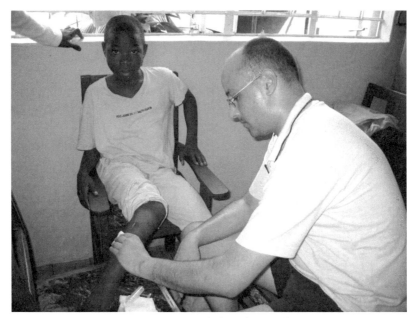

Simon treating infected wounds

Simon playing with the children

Soon it was time to return home, and I had to leave them in the hands of people I hoped I could trust.

By now, word had got around at home in England and people were beginning to get more involved.

Simon was brilliant and had used his skills to treat the children's infected wounds, taking pictures and playing with them. They were fascinated with his camera as they had never seen one before and couldn't believe it when they saw themselves looking back at them! He is desperate to return to Sierra Leone, and I have promised to take him.

It wasn't long after my return home that someone suggested I officially start a charity for these dear children, but I still had my business to consider.

Nevertheless, I began the long process of registering a charity with the charity commission, which took many months, as well as continuing to honour my work with my brides, many of whom had now become involved with what I was doing in Africa, and often did fundraising events.

They used to ask to see the photos of the children on my return, so I put together an album for them to look at when they came for their wedding dress fittings.

As I reflected, I had done extremely well in my business and had achieved my goals, but I knew that something had to change, and it wasn't everyone who could go out to Africa and do what I was doing.

Each time I returned to Sierra Leone, it became harder and harder to devote my time to both my business and the needy children in Sierra Leone. I also had to step back from Rotary as I couldn't do everything.

It took me another three years to finally make the decision and take a huge step of faith to close my successful business and devote my life entirely to helping these orphans and abandoned street children in Sierra Leone.

Chapter 3
The Charity Is Born

I was sitting in the airport waiting for my flight home, on one occasion, when a man came up to me and asked what I was doing in his country? His name was John Malamah-Thomas. He was from Sierra Leone but was now living in London with his wife and daughter.

I told him my story of how I became involved and working in 'his country' and his reaction was: "Well if you're doing all this for my people, what am I doing?" He offered to help me with the many contacts he had in Sierra Leone. He said he'd be in touch when he had some more information, which he duly did, and he was an amazing support to me.

As a result of people hearing about what I was doing, through local newspaper articles, they got in touch and wanted to do more.

We all agreed to have a meeting and decided to form a committee. Different people had different jobs within the committee, and it worked well. They, in turn, shared the story and it soon began to mushroom. It wasn't long before we had willing sponsors and I decided to put £10,000 of my own money in to get it started.

An elderly lady I knew, called Sylvia Lee, had actually lived in Sierra Leone for many years with her husband who went out as a teacher. Three of their four daughters were born in Sierra Leone, and she was on the committee. It was through her that we named the charity 'The Cotton Tree Children's Trust'. This was after the huge cotton tree that sits in the centre of Freetown, the capital of Sierra Leone.

Slaves were freed there many years ago and it was thought that it would be appropriate for our children. They would now be free from a life of poverty and be given new hope for a better future.

According to some sources, the Cotton Tree is 500 years old. It is believed that when a group of former African American slaves, who had gained their freedom by fighting for the British during the American War of Independence, landed in Freetown, they apparently rested and prayed underneath the shade of the tree.

The Cotton Tree in the centre of Freetown

In 2005, there was a big event in London called BBC Africa Live and John Malamah Thomas invited me to go. I met with Gordon Brown, then the Chancellor of the Exchequer, and Sir Bob Geldof.

I wasn't too impressed with Sir Bob's crumpled linen suit, but I let that go, as he was very taken with what I was doing. He said that if you really believe in your heart about what you are doing, then keep going!

BBC Africa Live in London with Gordon Brown and Sir Bob Geldof in 2005

I continued to go out to Sierra Leone and work with the child mothers and other street children. I took out an old Singer sewing machine and, can you believe, I took it on the plane as hand luggage!

By now, the checking-in desk at Heathrow had got to know me and very kindly allowed me an extra 10 kilos of luggage to take out for the charity.

I taught the older girls how to sew, as they could go on to do tailoring. I also taught the children to read and write, and especially to learn English, which was their second language.

Abi learning to sew on a machine

Teaching Frances English

Life is very different out there as were most other activities, such as bathing the children in a large washing up bowl! Abandoned children also slept outside on benches.

Washing and cleaning teeth!

Abandoned street children sleeping rough

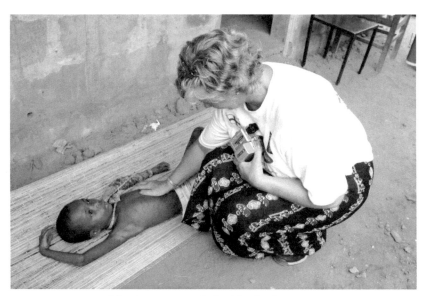
Nursing a young lad with a broken arm

As well as working with the child mothers and other children, I would go out into the streets to see other children desperately needing help. Many children were sleeping rough with no home, no parents, and no hope for a future. I would also see sick children who had broken limbs with no hope of ever getting the correct medical help, like the little boy above who had broken his arm. There was no such luxury as plaster of Paris to set his arm.

Chapter 4
Finding Our New Home

After a lot of heart-searching on my return home to England, I decided it was time to find our own home for the children I was going to rescue from social welfare. This was in order to officially start and register our charity in Sierra Leone.

I went back out to look for suitable premises to rent. I remember standing in a derelict building from the war thinking, *What am I doing? This is such a huge responsibility laying on my shoulders.* I can only say that it was my faith that had brought me this far, and it would be my faith that would carry me through.

This is the bungalow we finally decided to rent. It was owned by a local dentist and his family who had fled during the civil war and had not returned. It needed work doing on it but nothing that could not be put right. It was infested with cockroaches in the cupboards and the doors were falling off, but that didn't deter me. With the help of John Malamah-Thomas or JMT – as we called him – and his friends, we soon got it up together.

JMT and Rosemary at our new home

Building the outside kitchen

Our finished outside kitchen

I then interviewed and employed a manager to oversee the running of our home whilst I was back in England, and housemothers who would care for our children, do all the cooking and the children's washing.

They were all so lovely and could hardly believe how lucky they were to be given a job.

The new manager far left and our house mothers

Aunty Elizabeth in our new kitchen

Chapter 5
Things Don't Always Go as Planned

Sadly, the organisation I had entrusted to look after Abi and little Rosie, Frances, and little Mohammed, let me down badly and forced Abi and Frances back on the streets with their babies.

The 'organisation' had been set up by a 40-year-old English man, who I later discovered was paying extortionate amounts of money to a local woman he put in charge whilst he went back to England. He had no idea of where this money was going.

The first I knew of what had happened was when I had a call from a friend of Abi's saying she was very sick and had been mistreated and needed help urgently.

I was due to fly out soon anyway, so I brought my flight forward and flew out to try and find them.

When I arrived in Freetown, I, along with friends began to look for them. We called on some more friends, but still, we had no joy after three days of searching. Then, to my horror, I was greeted by the police who had come to arrest me, supposedly, for child trafficking!

I was horrified and had to spend a week being interrogated by the police in the main police station in Freetown. They seized my passport and were relentless in their questioning.

The organisation to which I had entrusted Abi and little Rosie, Frances, and little Mohammed, had bribed the police about a year's salary to do this. They knew that if I ever asked Abi, she would tell me how she, Frances and the other children in their care were being mistreated.

Then one day, whilst I was being detained at the police station, Abi came out of the blue to find me as she had received word about what had happened. The first thing we did was to get her medical help.

I could hardly believe my eyes and broke down. She wiped away my tears with the hem of her long dusty skirt and said, "Don't worry, Mum, I'll look after you." She then began to explain what had happened and said that whenever this 'organisation' had word that visitors were coming, mainly from England, the woman who was put in charge would go out into the streets and bring children in, bribing them with money. They would be bribed and told to lie to the visitors and of course, the visitors believed them and would give the woman in charge money…a lot of money. So much so that she was able to buy herself an old BMW car!

I couldn't believe what they had done, especially after everything I had done for them previously.

At one stage, the police said I could go free if I promised never to return to Freetown or Sierra Leone.

I wasn't going to agree to do that! I had made those child mothers and their babies a promise, when they were christened, that I would never leave them or forsake them, and I wasn't about to break my promise, so I stuck it out!

So enraged was this 'organisation' that they even went to the newspapers, and I was front-page news!

JMT (John Malamah-Thomas) and his friends made frantic phone calls to everyone they knew in high places. John knew that if I were found guilty, I would be locked up in prison and would probably only last about three days.

So desperate was he that he decided to get up early one morning and wait to see the High Court Judge who always went for a run along Lumley beach. He managed to see him and explained that I was this wonderful white woman who had given up everything to go out to his country and rescue orphans and street children and give them a new life.

The Judge stopped running as he took in what was being said. Later that day, in the highest court in Freetown, my case was heard. The judge listened to all the evidence brought against me by this 'organisation' and dismissed it out of hand, saying that as they, the 'organisation' had thrown Abi out onto the streets, and had abducted Rosie and kept her hidden. It was them who were in breach of the law, not me. The judge said, "It was simply impossible for Rosemary to have been seen running off with a 16-year-old called Abi under one arm and Rosie under the other." This was as the newspapers had reported!

I was completely exonerated, and the case was dropped, it ended up with the police investigating the 'organisation' in question, finding them guilty of running an illegal organisation for street children without proper documentation or court orders for the children they used from the streets!

Feeling very traumatised, I asked for my passport back from the police so I could return home, and they refused. It is unreal at times! I ended up having to pay them to get my passport back!

I returned home on the next available flight after I made sure Abi was being medically looked after, and little Rosie was safe in the hands of dear friends who had supported me so much.

Having thought that I was cleared of all charges, I flew back to Heathrow.

It wasn't until I came to go through Customs that I became aware of a problem. I showed my passport as normal and the man behind the desk looked at me, looked at my passport, then back at me, and said, "Wait here."

He came back and asked me to follow him. We went into a room where the table and chairs were chained to the floor. What on earth was going on! What had I done wrong?

It then became clear that, as a result of my arrest which led to the hearing in the High Court, there was a problem with my passport as it showed that I was involved in a case with 'minors', and children being trafficked!

So there I sat trying as hard as I knew how to explain what had happened. After a couple of hours of being detained, they finally let me go!

But to my horror, every time I tried to get back into the UK, the same thing happened. Every time it flagged up on my passport and every time I was detained until eventually, I had to contact my local MP to ask for help.

After a suitably worded letter from my MP, amazingly, my passport was cleared, but every time I came back to the UK, my heart missed a beat as I wait for my passport to be given back to me!

Chapter 6
A Holiday Like No Other

Our new orphanage was still not quite ready inside so Abi and Rosie had nowhere to go until it was finished and were still unwell, so in 2006, I began the process of trying to bring Abi and little Rosie back to England so I could get them better. This was both costly and fraught with problems, but with the help of friends in Freetown, we somehow managed it!

They both had passports, visas, and all other paperwork, and with the support of the British Embassy and one of my friends who got them to the airport, they flew for the very first time. Abi was just sixteen and little Rosie was just two years old.

I drove to Heathrow to meet them and could hardly contain myself. Then finally saw this frail thin young girl carrying a small child walking towards me through arrivals. I had done it against all the odds.

They came with what they stood up in and that was their entire world.

I drove them home and they were dazed with everything around them. What a complete contrast for them, just as it was for me the first time I set foot on African soil.

I had made up a double bed so they could sleep together. The picture of them sleeping was priceless. I didn't want to go to bed myself, and just wanted to soak up the wonder of this moment and what we had been through and achieved together. They were both very thin and malnourished, so I use to weigh them each week to see how much weight they were putting on. It wasn't long before they both looked so much better and happier, and become more confident.

Abi and Rosie fast asleep

Rosie surrounded with her new toys

People soon got to hear of our new arrivals and came bearing gifts for both Rosie and Abi. The first things they needed were shoes and clothes, so off we went to see what we could find. Everywhere we went, people stopped and admired these two beautiful children. When we went to Sainsbury's, Abi just loved walking up and down the isles on her own, feeling very important. Rosie would sit in the trolley waving at everyone as they went by, saying 'Good morning', or 'Good afternoon' and would simply melt the hearts of everyone they met. Gradually, I could see them blossom into two beautiful children.

As I had done the gala dinner with Sir Norman Wisdom, he was very interested in meeting these two beautiful girls and came to my house to meet them. He couldn't put Rosie down and I think he would have eaten her if he could! It was so lovely to see.

Sir Norman Wisdom and the girls in my garden in 2006

People would say, "Are you going to spoil them and take them to lots of lovely places?"

"No," I replied, "because it would be too confusing for them."

But I did take them to the zoo so they could see the animals for the first time. Since the civil war, there were no animals left in Sierra Leone as the rebels had either killed them or eaten them! They had never seen horses, or elephants, or any other animal. Their faces were a picture!

I also took them to see my mother in the car, which was a two-hour drive away. They loved it just as much as my mum loved them. Rosie was particularly fascinated with my mum's electric piano, so here she is below entertaining us all!

Rosie on my mother's lap

Rosie playing my mother's piano

Abi and Rosie in the park and Rosie playing with the toys in a garden centre in 2006

Sylvia Lee, who use to live in Freetown, and the girls with myself and Sir Norman

Three months later, I had to return Abi and Rosie and put them on the plane back to Sierra Leone where they stayed with friends until I could return a few weeks later for Christmas and get our rented home renovated for our first intake of children in 2007. They always knew they would return to their homeland, and that they would see me again very soon.

Chapter 7
2007 Our First Ten Children

In June 2007, I went out to Sierra Leone with the sole purpose of rescuing our first ten orphans and abandoned street children and bringing them into our new home.

I will never forget it. I sat in a very hot and humid room at Social Welfare for many long hours trying to work out from all the children who were the most vulnerable. I felt that it was more important to rescue the youngest and sickest, but I didn't want to split up the siblings.

How do you choose which child to take as Social Welfare had so many that needed help? It was a feeling that I will never forget. All of them looked so sad and sick, but I had to somehow choose just ten.

I had chosen the ninth child and by this time, I was really tired and drained emotionally. I felt that I should settle for these nine, but then suddenly a young boy was brought back in for me to see. I couldn't work it out as I had already seen him, but he said he was with his two older brothers.

I asked him if he was an orphan and why he was with the other boys, and he said he thought that I would take him in if he said he was the brother of the others! His name was Momoh. My heart melted for him and said, "Momoh, you are a very lucky boy; so I am going to call you my lucky number ten!" His face lit up as he realised how fortunate he was. Ever since that day, he has been known as number ten. So when I have called them on the phone to talk to them all, I couldn't always recognise their voices, but when I asked which one he was, he always answered, "I'm your number ten, Grandma!"

I slowly made my way home with a heavy heart, thinking about all the other children that I couldn't take in.

Three days later, I returned to give these poor dear children a new home and a new life. They all walked out to the vehicle and there was a deadly hush as they climbed in one at a time.

One little boy called Hassan just screamed and screamed at me as he held a bottle of water. He hadn't seen a white woman before so close-up!

Sitting in the vehicle with them all, I suddenly became very aware of the overwhelming responsibility I had taken on. These children now depended totally and utterly on me for their every need. This wasn't just going to be for the short-term; this was going to be for the rest of their lives!

We made our way along the potholed dusty roads to our new home. There they got out, looking around to see where I had brought them. By this time, I had the new housemothers I had employed waiting to greet them.

They all walked up the steps and into their new home. I had bought new bunk beds, mattresses, and bedsheets, as well as a table and chairs to eat our meals and for all the children to do their schoolwork. The outside kitchen was now all equipped with pots and pans for everything they needed to cook with. The inside kitchen had plastic cups and plates for them to eat from.

We settled them in and gave them their first proper meal to warm their tummies before bedtime. It must have been overwhelming for them too as they had not experienced anything like this before. Soon, it was time for bed, but what I hadn't realised was that they had never slept in a bed, let alone bunk beds! This was all a bit much for them and they didn't understand about going up this little wooden ladder to sleep on the top bunk! So in the end, we put their mattresses on the floor for them and they slept two, three and sometimes four across these mattresses.

The little ones were still not sure, so I lay down on one of the mattresses with them and held them all in my arms until they fell fast asleep. This was such a precious moment for me. The first time I had all these little lives in my arms. I didn't want to leave them.

I had finally done it! I had achieved my first goal.

Saffie Kanga, one of our first children

The first orphans I took in in June 2007

Some of the boys sleeping on the mattress

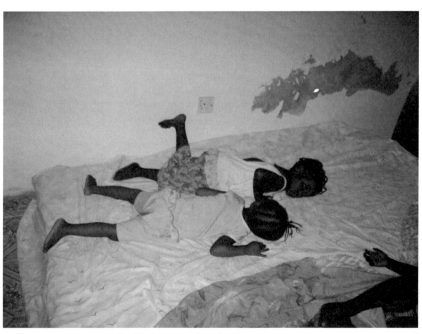

The little ones sleeping on mattresses

The sad faces of the first ten children I had rescued in June 2007

When we had settled the children in our new home, Abi wanted to go and find her friend, Frances, who had a baby at the same time as Abi, so we set off to find her. Abi said she thought she might be living in the slums of the lorry park. It was a very deprived area of Freetown and one that men would go to and pay girls for sex. Abi and I set off to see if we could find her. It was bad enough for locals to be there, but for me, a white woman, it was very risky, but I knew Abi would protect me. It was very intimidating, but I knew I had to do this for Frances.

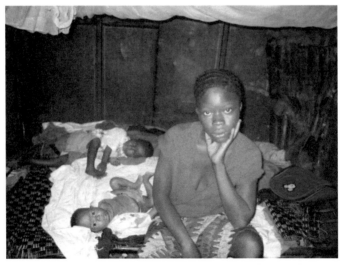
Frances with her two little boys and no hope for any future

The happy face of Frances when we gave her a new home

We eventually found Frances in an old shack with a cloth for a front door. I couldn't even see inside as it was so dark, but Abi assured me it was Frances, and not only with Mohammed but also with a new baby too, called Alimamy, that had been born in the lorry park with no idea who the father was. The only way I could see them was to put the flash on with my camera. It broke my heart to see where she had ended up as a result of being pushed out onto the streets by the 'organisation' that promised to care for her. It was hard to take in what was before my eyes. Abi spoke to her to reassure her, and Frances said she thought I had abandoned her, as I didn't come looking for her.

I reminded her of the promise I had made both of them when their babies were christened. I asked her if she would like to come and live in our new home with her two little boys. The transformation on her face said everything! She smiled with excitement and knew she would be safe and have a future for her two boys.

Our home had now become the 'Home of Inner Happiness'.

Mohammed and Alimamy in our new home

Alimatu feeding her sick sister

This was the first day of their new lives! They had never seen toys, so it was all a bit strange, but at least they were safe and had clean water to drink and proper food in their tummies.

Leaving these dear children was going to be so hard as I had just got to know them. They were all so vulnerable. There were many tears, but the one thing the children clung to was that I would return to see them very soon to officially open our new home in October.

I returned as planned to open our home. The welcome was overwhelming! And the children were simply unrecognisable! In just a few short months, they had been transformed from very malnourished, frightened little children to bright, happy little people who had been given a new life.

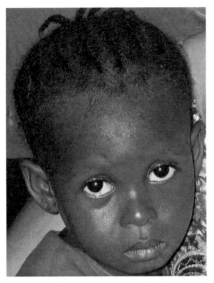 

Saffie Kanga June 2007   Saffie Kanga October 2007

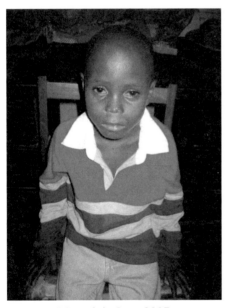 

Momoh in June 2007   Momoh in October 2007

The transformation was unbelievable.

Chapter 8
The Opening of Our New Home

The opening of our new home

One big happy family

The day had finally come! I was about to officially open our new home for these dear orphans and abandoned street children. I could hardly believe what I had achieved! This was going to be a day I would never forget!

We had invited friends and special people from Freetown and the pastor who conducted the service. I chose the hymns, which meant a lot to me, and reflected what we had achieved.

I was struck as the pastor gave his address, in which he said that it was worse to be abandoned than to be orphaned. This meant that someone had made a conscious decision to give their child up, or just walk away and leave that child abandoned for someone else to take in because they couldn't afford to care for it. It's hard for us to comprehend how a mother could do this and simply walk away, but life is so different out there. Everything comes down to one thing – survival. There was a plaque I used to see, which read, 'To live till death is a struggle.'

Often the women would have been raped, or sold their bodies for sex to get money, usually for just £1!

We can't begin to imagine what it was like for them to give birth in such dreadful circumstances, then to walk away from their babies, as you knew you had no money to feed it! That was why I was often given babies by their mothers, as they knew they would have a better chance of life if I took them in.

It broke my heart not to be able to take everyone in, but I had to think with my head, as well as my heart. I would revisit them in the lorry park every time I returned to give them food and much-needed medicines. It was better to give them food rather than money as that was often stolen from them.

I had bought some ribbon from our local shop in Warwick with the colours of the Sierra Leone flag. Blue for the sea, green for the forests, and white for the sky.

We tied them across the front door and then, at the appropriate time, I cut them to officially open our new home. I was so full of emotion I could hardly see through my tears.

I could hardly believe what I had achieved through sheer determination.

All the children were wearing their special Africana outfits we had made for them, and one by one, they walked up the steps and into their new home! A moment I will never forget. There was much merriment with music, food, and wonderful speeches! I had achieved my goal. Life was never the same after this.

We settled down into what was now their new home, and a new way of life before I had to fly back to England.

It felt very strange as I boarded the plane once again. I looked around and wondered what was going through other people's minds? What had they achieved on their visit to Freetown? I'm sure they would not have experienced what I had and reminded myself of the words someone used when giving a lecture about self-determination and triumph over adversity when they talked about 'the power of one'! I returned to see them about every three months.

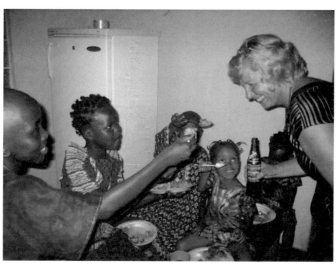

Chapter 9
Our Second Intake of Children

In June 2008, I returned to rescue another eight children. It was lovely to see the children I had rescued the year before. They had become very close and called each other 'brothers and sisters'.

I went through the same process as I had done the year before.

Each one of them with a desperate need to be loved and given another chance of life. I knew I couldn't take them all. My aim on this visit was to take in another eight children as I knew I had enough funding for them.

A family of three children were brought before me. Their father was dead, and their mother had just died within the last three days. They looked so sad and lost, and the elder one carried her younger brother on her back as he was only two years old. What was I to do? I went back to my room and thought long and hard about these three young children. I had a choice, to take just two and leave one of them, not to take any of them, or to take in all three siblings…I did the latter and with my faith, I knew I would somehow find a sponsor to support them.

The three siblings I chose to take in

The second intake of children in 2008

All of our children together as one big happy family in 2008

One of our sponsors had written the following in their church magazine:

"In four short years, The Cotton Tree Trust had grown from an idea in Rosemary's head to an organised, official charity with a home, staff and, to date, 18 children. No one who has seen the 'then and now' photographs of those children can fail to be moved by the contrast. Their frightened, forlorn, and empty expressions on arrival to their new home had been transformed and they were now happy, joyful and well-adjusted children who feel safe and know love.

For the first time in their short lives, they are receiving an education. We are all familiar with Rosemary's selfless commitment to her charity and we cannot fail to have been moved by her enthusiasm and the emotive reports she gives us. Rosemary was a successful and prosperous businesswoman who gave up her career to devote her life to these children of The Cotton Tree Children's Trust. The charity is funded entirely from donations, individual sponsorships and fund-raising events. All money donated goes towards food, education and healthcare for the children." Written by Hayward.

On my return to the home from rescuing our second intake of children, I tried once again to get back into 'normal life', whatever 'normal' was now.

I set off and went to my regular weekly dancing lessons, looking suntanned as I always did on my returns from Africa, when someone called Martin Evans asked me where I had been on my holidays, suggesting it would be somewhere exotic! When I told him where I had been, he was visibly taken aback! "What on earth were you doing going out there?" he asked.

I proceeded to tell him, giving the potted version, and explaining how I had just returned from taking in more children.

It turned out that Martin had found himself at a bit of a crossroads in life and wanted to know more. We arranged a meeting so I could show him the video and pictures of the work I had been doing. Visibly moved, Martin offered there and then to sponsor the three siblings I had just taken in! That was an answer to my prayer!

At the time, Martin was working for Jaguar Land Rover and decided he would ask permission to do some fund-raising at work.

He arranged a cycling event around the six-mile test tack on which they usually tested their cars. He also had static bikes indoors! It was a brilliant success and raised over £1,800. Enough to feed and care for our children for three months!

Then came another idea from Martin. To do a skydive! He'd got sponsors and had T-shirts made for us all, so four of us went off to Oxford one sunny August day and jumped out of a plane!

One was sick, one was terrified, (that was me), and the other two loved it!

The four of us before we jumped out

Rosemary with her certificate

Martin decided he wanted to become more involved and became a valuable committee member and real support.

I was due to return to see the children in December of that year, and Martin said he wanted to come out to see for himself the work I was doing.

Having been in the RAF as an engineer, he could turn his hand to most things, which would be a great help to me in the home.

The day came for us to fly out, but this time I had another passenger. As our plane touched down and we walked down the steps onto the tarmac in the warm humid night air, a voice inside said, "Welcome home once again." We began the now familiar hustle and bustle and fight to get our luggage from the makeshift conveyor belt and join the usual chaotic frenzy to get outside in the pitch dark. We had to try and find our way to the clapped-out helicopter, which was to take us across the water from Lungi airport to the mainland of Freetown.

What I hadn't mentioned was those three days before my last trip, twenty-two people, most of them Togolese sports officials, were killed when the passenger helicopter exploded and crashed at Lungi airport, Sierra Leone's main international airport, where I was now standing!

I will never forget the image of the green tarpaulin covering the bodies and wreckage still lying on the tarmac, and here was I about to board the only helicopter and mode of transport to get us to the other side! I was terrified, but for Martin, this was a great adventure. I wished I could have shared his excitement!

I had explained what happened before but as an engineer and ex-RAF, he assured me that this sparkly new white helicopter was going to be okay.

I double-checked with staff that this plane was safe, and of course, they gave me the answer they wanted me to hear!

With as much reassurance as I could get, we both climbed aboard the helicopter. There were no seat belts and no glass in the windows! So there wasn't much to protect us if this thing were to land in the sea! We all sat on the bench seats along the sides, and our luggage was piled high in the middle of us all. As the rotor blades started up, this was the point of no return. My heart was in my mouth, but there was nothing I could do, but just go with it!

Martin, on the other hand, was seeing this as a real experience and enjoyed every minute!

Before long, we reached the other side and touched down safely. Phew! I have to say I was very thankful to have my feet firmly on the ground! It wasn't until about three days later that Martin told me that the only thing new on the helicopter was the white paint!

Someone was there to meet us, and it was so good to 'be home' again. The next day we set off to see the children in their new home.

We were given, the now familiar, warm welcome by the children, singing to us and flinging their arms around us with happiness.

A family had donated a trampoline for the children, which we had shipped out, so the children sat and watched while Martin put it together. He then showed them what to do by having a go and jumping on it first, much to their amusement! Even the housemothers had a go and thought it was hilarious!

We put the children on, one by one and they absolutely loved it! It was just so lovely to see them so happy and really enjoying themselves.

Our home was always in need of repairs due to the humid climate, and the lack of maintenance. The ceiling had wood bugs that damaged the ceilings and the doors. The water pipes needed maintaining as people used to cut our pipes from the main source outside our compound and attach their pipes onto ours and took our water!

Another job Martin did was to try and fix the fuse box so we could have light. We couldn't quite believe it when he put the lights on, especially after he almost electrocuted himself!

With twenty children and the dusty climate, it soon got grubby on the walls. Martin replaced the damaged sockets that had corroded and rewired areas that needed replacing. We didn't realise how bright it was until we switched on the new lights. Thanks to Martin! Everything looked so much brighter, and dirtier! We only had a small generator which we used for two hours at night so the children could do their homework.

Martin and the trampoline

Mending the fuse box

Life Goes On

We had been asked to go and visit the lorry park, which is where Abi and Rosie lived when I first met them in 2004. It's an area on the east side of Freetown, called Kissy, where hundreds of people were killed during the civil war.

It's a very poor area and many children barely survive in these filthy alleyways.

On my visits, I had come to know the children living there. I would take them food, as I knew they would benefit from that the most. When I first went to the lorry park, I found it very intimidating as a white woman and I was viewed with great suspicion. Martin also felt the intimidation. On this occasion, we had taken them some treats and sweets, which they loved as well as biscuits. On one occasion, I was given twin babies only a few months old and asked to take them in as the mother didn't have any money to look after them. Sadly, I couldn't take them as we didn't have enough room or sponsors for anymore, but I did go back every time to see them and their mother and give them much needed food and medicines.

Whilst we were out there, Abi became very ill with malaria and typhoid. She had been taken into hospital two weeks before we had flown out with the same thing and was so weak she couldn't fight the disease. We put her in the back of our vehicle and took her to the hospital. She stayed there for some time until we eventually decided to bring her home with her drip, as she was not in the cleanest place in the hospital. I attached her drip onto the small window latch high up in a bedroom and sat with her constantly just praying she would recover. Rosie sat by her side looking completely lost and bewildered.

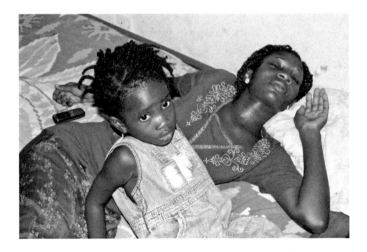

As each day went by, Abi got a little bit stronger until she eventually recovered. All the children were very vulnerable to infections and don't have a good immune system. I was struck by the number of our children who were sick each time I went out.

We had weekly meetings with the housemothers to improve the children's diet, but despite their frequent illnesses, they were doing remarkably well at school. They were just so hungry to learn. One of our boys came top in his year, and Rosie, aged four, came first in her nursery class!

Not bad for children who had no hope of any future!

Christmas 2008

People would often ask me, "Do they know it's Christmas?" Yes, they know it's Christmas, but they don't know the joy and happiness it brings as our children do.

Along with the trampoline, we had shipped out Christmas shoeboxes for all the children.

There was a little boy called Michael, aged about nine who lived on the streets with his mum and brother, Anthony. He would stand and watch us through the railings. One day, he asked if he could help us sort the Christmas shoeboxes. I asked him, "Do you receive anything at Christmas?"

"No," he replied.

As he helped us put all the shoeboxes in the vehicle to take to the children, I said, "Would you like to come with us and have one of these shoeboxes as your Christmas present?" His face lit up with a big beaming smile.

"Yes please," he said. He jumped into the vehicle amongst all the shoeboxes and came with us to see the children. He helped unload them all, including a big plastic bag with something red in it!

I had shipped out a Father Christmas outfit for Martin to wear to give out the shoeboxes, but I'd forgotten how hot it would be! The children's faces were priceless! And Martin, he was sweltering underneath the white hair and beard!

One by one, they came forward to receive a shoebox from Father Christmas. They just sat and looked at it as much to say, 'what do I do now?' They all looked at one another and then at us. We said, "You can open it!" They still looked very confused as they opened up the boxes. This wasn't the reaction we were expecting! They sat motionlessly. Did they not like their presents? What was the problem? They had never been given anything in their lives before so therefore they didn't know how to react. The children were overwhelmed and could only ever have dreamt of something like this happening to them.

They had never experienced the excitement of being given a present. We had to explain that the things in their shoeboxes were presents from their sponsors and an infant school in Warwick...And yes, even Michael and his little brother, Anthony, had a shoebox as well!

All of us including the staff and JMT

After the New Year, we had a personal invitation to the Presidential State House to meet with the President of Sierra Leone, Mr Ernest Koroma. We were the only white people there, so we drew a bit of attention to the proceedings.

He was giving a presentation to ex-patriots, encouraging them to return to their homeland and invest in the economy to rebuild their country. We were very privileged to be publicly acknowledged by the President for our work with orphans and abandoned street children in his homeland. The First Lady even invited our children to her big garden party she put on each year for children.

Left, John Malamah-Thomas, Rosemary Bidwell and President Ernest Koroma

A Treat to The Beach

The beaches in Sierra Leone are amazing and the children love to dress up in their Sunday best clothes to go to the beach! We hired a mini-bus, and along with the housemothers and the big bowls of rice and food for the day, we all piled in and off we went! As I turned and looked at them all on the bus, happily singing, I was reminded of the day I rescued them all and took them to their new home to begin a new life. The overwhelming responsibility was immense as I took them from a life of poverty with no hope of any future, to a life of hope and happiness.

I had bought them all swimming costumes and it wasn't long before they started playing in the sand and wanting to go in the sea. Have you ever tried taking eighteen excited children swimming! None of them could swim so they were bobbing up and down like corks! I had to keep counting them just to make sure we had them all! They absolutely loved it and it was wonderful to see them enjoying themselves.

Bintu loving the water

61

A friend of mine had put us up in his hotel and gave Martin one of the best rooms to say thank you to him, but it was about to be handed over to the United Nations. So each day, there was less and less food, less and less people and furniture until one morning there was just Martin and I and no food, not even an egg for breakfast, so we had to eat some of the fizzy sweets we had bought for the children to keep us going!

Soon, it was time once again for us to say farewell. I had got to know our children so much more, that it made it that much harder to leave them. So with very heavy hearts, we packed our suitcases once more and made our way up to the home.

The children were now familiar with the sound of our vehicle, but unlike every other time we drove to the home, they didn't come rushing out to greet us.

We drove into the compound and one by one, they came up to us, giving us big hugs and kisses with tears rolling down their faces.

It's so hard to say goodbyes. Little did they realise that behind our sunglasses, we too had tears of sadness.

It had been another emotional journey. These dear children had taken another piece of my heart, and I loved them so much more now.

As we were driven to the airport, there was a deadly silence. There were no words to describe the feelings, just the immense privilege that I have been given to care for these young lives.

So until the next time, I continued to work tirelessly doing presentations, charity events and anything else I could think of to raise money for these dear children.

Chapter 10
Life Goes On

On another dancing occasion, I met a man called Alan Daley, and once again, I'd returned from three months in Freetown, suntanned.

By now, word had got around the dance class about this crazy woman who kept going out to Africa and had set up a home for orphans and street children! Alan wanted to know more about the work I was doing, just like Martin.

A few months later, as I was preparing to go back out on another trip in January 2010, Alan asked, "How many will there be going out in the team?"

"Er, that will be just one! Me!"

He then asked if he could come with me? Like Martin, he was very good with DIY and could turn his hand to most things, so he would be a real asset to me out there. It was important for me to vet and assess who I took out to establish if they were able to cope. It was stressful enough and, apart from which, the locals would seize the chance to rob anyone who was white who didn't look confident.

Once briefed, and having had all his inoculations, Alan was ready for the life-changing adventure.

Alan has three sons and he asked if he could sponsor two little sisters and has done so for many years. They have definitely benefitted from his financial support.

Martin, realising how difficult it was to get around when he came out, decided to look for a vehicle for us, so went online and made a bid on eBay for a Nissan Terrano 4x4 and got it for £500!

He spent all his spare time doing it up and making it roadworthy before we shipped it out! We decided to fill it up with all sorts of necessary things for the children but were not given the correct advice from someone we trusted and sadly, when it arrived in Sierra Leone, it was completely empty!

All the children's presents from their sponsors had gone along with bags of sheets and towels and many other things we had shipped out. I was heartbroken. I felt I'd let so many people down, especially the children and their sponsors. Alan set about sorting out the damaged vehicle, putting it back together again for me to drive, but minus all the children's presents!

Our eBay 4x4 ready to be shipped out

I had now got my Sierra Leone driving licence, which made things so much easier to get around. That was an achievement in itself. It took many hours in a friend's vehicle, stuck in traffic in searing heat, that by the time I reached the Department of Transport, my cotton dress was stuck to me as if I'd just got out of the shower! I then had to repeat all this a second time to go and collect my licence.

The queues for the 26-year-old taxis were 200 deep at times, just to get into town, which could take two hours or more to do the five-mile journey.

Our old Nissan Terrano was a godsend. Just one of the many things we take for granted here in the UK.

It really was a struggle, so to have our own 4x4 made it possible to achieve all the things we had to do on each visit including taking the children to the beach!

Happiness at the beach

Our children had learnt how invaluable their sponsors were to them and always asked how they were. They are the children's lifelines!

One of the highlights of our trip was to take the children to the beach. They got so excited and would count the number of sleeps until we went just like English children. It was wonderful to see them all enjoying themselves and playing in the sea. It was quite a challenge, as not many people I know would be brave enough to take all our children under thirteen in the sea!

People in Sierra Leone are taught to fear the sea because of its strong currents, so it was important for me to teach the children how to swim and not fear it.

We were still having to sleep in B&Bs as there wasn't enough room in our home, so I gave Alan what was the 'best' room! Mine was down the corridor and nowhere near as good. The first morning after we had arrived, I asked Alan how he had slept? He said he didn't and showed me his pillow, which appeared to have a family of insects living in it! I guess I had become used to things like this. I wasn't happy and asked for a different pillow for him.

Another trip was in November 2010. This was the second time I had taken out two committee members at the same time. It was indeed progress and would certainly spread the word of what we had achieved.

As we touched down on African soil, it had that now-familiar warm air smell of 'home'.

Once again, the children gave us their usual warm welcome and a wonderful presentation of singing and dancing which never failed to disappoint!

Our two visitors were very moved by this. One was Alan Daley, who I had taken out a few months earlier. He had now become the committee chairman and great support to me as he had been out with me and seen first-hand the issues being raised.

The children had all grown much taller and were now showing greater signs of their personalities. They were a lot more confident and open and displayed large amounts of affection to us as well as still needing that reassurance too.

They were all doing really well at school and the two little boys, Ibrahim and Alimamy, were really enjoying their first taste of school life! They were so conscientious and loved to spend time writing the letters of the alphabet and drawing pictures. They were especially taking part in the homework programme I set up after school on the veranda of our home, where one of the housemothers would do English with them on the blackboard.

Much had improved since our last visit with our housemothers providing better diets, growing our green vegetables, and even building a chicken run in the compound!

They went to the market to buy these chickens and brought them back under their arms! All was going well, and the children were able to have fresh eggs until apparently 'the daddy chicken became troublesome, and they decided they had to eat him!'

I took the committee member 'Hillary' (not her real name) who had not been out to Freetown before, to visit the Princess Christian maternity hospital in Kissy, as she had wanted to go and see it. This was quite an eye-opener. We saw young mothers who had travelled many miles to get there and been in labour for hours or sometimes, days. Some had lost their babies giving birth or were suffering extreme injuries, and some were simply not going to make it at all.

I became aware of her talking to staff members about what she was hoping to do. I realised that she had been in communication with them in some depth before our visit. However, we continued our visit around the hospital until it was time to leave.

As we were over in that part of town, I decided to take 'Hillary' to the lorry park where I first met the young child mothers, Abi, and Frances, whilst working there some years before. It was still quite intimidating as a white woman, but they have learnt to trust me.

Mothers came out of tin shacks carrying their babies where you simply couldn't see in. Again, we had bought food and biscuits for the children. All we could see was a sea of hands reaching out for food.

One little boy, about eight years old, was carrying a young child and he was so desperate for food, he grabbed the bag of crumbs and began to run, but he stumbled and fell in the gutter and dropped the child.

My heart missed a beat as I ran to pick the baby girl up and make sure she was not too hurt before giving her back. I suddenly realised how desperate these dear children were for food.

I had heard of a child who had been killed simply trying to get a sweet. Now, I could see for myself how true that was.

'Hillary' had enjoyed her first taste of Africa and coped very well with what had to be done, and despite my concerns with the hospital visit, I thought I had a good co-worker who could give me the support I needed on our return to the UK.

However, having devoted a lot of valuable time to her in Freetown, I was surprised on our return home to receive her letter of resignation to the committee, saying 'she needed to devote more time to her family'.

I was taken aback by this as she had really played an important part.

Sometime later, I was told that she had set up her charity with the help of the maternity hospital I had taken her to and was now going out to Freetown on a regular basis.

Alan Daley was far from happy, as he knew how much time and effort, I had put into making her feel welcome. It wasn't easy, but I had to accept that at least, she was doing something for others in Freetown.

Chapter 11
On the Move to a Bigger Home

The children were now growing up fast and as such needed more space, so on our next trip, we set about looking for a bigger home with more bedrooms.

Up until now, there was nowhere for us to stay with the children, so we had to have Bed and Breakfast accommodation, but not as we know it!

I remember, one occasion, when Alan and I went out and we were shown our rooms! I decided to give him the better looking one, which supposedly had a working shower and toilet, whilst I took the room down the corridor with nothing but an old bed and mosquito net with holes in. I decided to sleep in my clothes, as they were already filthy from the journey to get there, so it didn't really matter!

In the morning, I went to check on Alan who showed me what could only be described as a family of insects living in his pillow! His so-called shower consisted of a big drum of water and a jug, and that was it! The toilet didn't flush of course, so again the bucket of water and jug were used to flush it!

I had to share the bathroom with others, and it was much the same as Alan's, except the mesh at the window to stop mosquitos coming in was torn, so they all decided to fly in and sit in the water drum where we had to take water to wash!

A friend came to collect us and couldn't believe how bad our accommodation was. She called her friend who worked for the prison to ask if we could stay with him, and thankfully he said yes! We packed our things, paid the money, and left.

It's surprising how important it is to have fresh water simply to wash and drink. The small things that we take for granted.

We knew we had to get a bigger home so we could always stay with the children when we went out. My ultimate goal was to live with the children when I visited, so I could always be there for them, day, and night, and to give support to the housemothers.

Alan was excellent with the children and showed them how to use tools to mend things. It was good for the children to have a father figure in their lives too as this was lacking.

Alan working with the younger children

We went up to the children's school to see how they were doing and to meet with their teachers. They all had glowing reports and I was extremely proud of them all.

One of the other things we always did was to get them all medically checked. This was a mammoth operation with all our children, but JMT (John Malamah-Thomas) had a sister who was a GP and offered to see our children for free if we took them to her surgery. So one Saturday morning, we all set off to town to see her. We filled the surgery and she kindly opened it just for us! All the children were extremely well, considering what they had been through, and it showed what a little love and care could do. They were now well on the road to being healthy children. I had changed their diet to include more fruits and to have fish a bit more often.

As there were no cows left after the war, they just had dried milk, so I increased this, as I didn't feel they were getting enough nutrients. Their diet was rice with cassava leaves, potato leaves, crane leaves, or groundnut stew, along with rice. They would buy fresh produce every day and walk at least five miles there and back to get it. This would take them many hours to prepare their daily food. They would sit outside on the ground and chop, slice and grind the spices to make their food.

Before long, it was time for us to say our goodbyes and return home once again. The children still used to get upset, but at least they knew it wouldn't be long before I would return.

I was feeling particularly weak by now, but this was not unusual. We worked very hard and long hours in searing heat.

By now, we had a new way of getting across the water to Lungi airport from Freetown. It was by water taxi. Much safer and cheaper than those awful helicopters, which were now all grounded thank goodness!

We made our long journey across the water to Lungi and sat and waited for our flight. I hadn't felt too well but as we boarded the plane, I began to feel even worse; I had already had malaria once, and knew the symptoms, despite taking malaria tablets.

By the end of the long flight back to Heathrow, I was feeling very unwell. Alan drove me back and as soon as I got home, I called my GP who sent me straight to hospital. I was immediately put into isolation, as I had returned from Africa.

As I lay there, I saw a black African male nurse walking towards me. "Hello," he said. "I hear you have just returned from Sierra Leone?"

"Yes," I replied.

He went to say, "My home is in Freetown, in Sierra Leone. I came here to study and to send money back to my family." Now, what are the chances of that happening? I knew I would be in good hands as he would be able to explain to the doctors what had happened to me. He then proceeded to speak in Krio, (which is their language) and was surprised to hear my reply in Krio!

As the days went by, I got stronger and was eventually allowed home once again to continue my work.

I remember, I took myself away to recover and stayed in Bed and Breakfast in Hampshire. At the bottom of their garden was 'The Garden Room'. It was perfect. It overlooked the woods where deer would come up to the window and was so peaceful. I rested there for a few days, before gradually going out for short walks up the lane and sitting on a bench overlooking the beautiful countryside. It was a good place to recharge my batteries before taking on the next challenge.

It had been my mission to try and find a bigger house to rent for the children. There were many houses that had been abandoned as people fled during the civil war with just the clothes, they stood up in.

But you get wise to people out there, and because I am white, I have learnt that they see 'pound notes' pinned to me in their eyes! So in order for me to negotiate a deal on anything, including renting a property, I had to send a friend to see if there was anywhere suitable for us at all. If I went, the price would immediately become greatly inflated.

She eventually found somewhere which was quite big, and meant that I could live with the children, and so could the others that I took out.

We began the negotiations, which took a long time. Nothing happens in a hurry in Africa! As we say…TIA, meaning 'This Is Africa!'

At the same time, I was also looking to move house in the UK. It had got very close to my moving date, and I, then, became aware that I was about to move two houses at the same time! Something I'd not recommend!

I remember, I had to give some form of ID to the estate agents for my house, and the only thing I had on me at the time was my Sierra Leone driving licence! This was a first for them and raised a few smiles, but it did the trick! My other ID happened to be with the solicitors that day!

I just managed to move into my new house before turning around and flying out to Freetown to move the children! I had kept a box of Freetown clothes close by, so I knew where it was when I moved!

Less than two weeks later, I was back in Freetown to start the process all over again and move the children. But this was not going to be so easy.

It was now June 2011, and the rainy season was upon us. Not the best time to move, but never mind!

We managed to get some cardboard boxes, and each child had to pack their belongings into it and put their name on them. All the pots and pans from the outside kitchen had to be packed up, along with the dismantling of the children's bunk beds and all the bedding. If you think moving in the UK is stressful, think again in Africa!

The house we were renting was thankfully just up the road, but to get there was another story!

It was now raining constantly and the open back lorry, which was due to help us move and take the furniture, couldn't get up our potholed roads, so we had to walk up carrying the things we could.

We had to wait three days before the lorry could reach us, so we had to make do and sleep on the floor till then.

Moving African style with one of our girls on UK crutches with a broken leg!

It took us over a week to move but we had done it! It was lovely to have more space for the children to run around in, with areas to study and have our meals too. They all loved their new surroundings and ran from one room to the other to see what they could find.

The girls had a big room, so it was divided between the older girls and the younger ones.

I remember seeing them all sorting out their clothes and finding new homes for everything. The four older girls had an area of their own and saw themselves in a mirror on the wall for the first time! Their faces were a picture. They felt like movie stars!

The boys were all in a room together down the corridor. There were only six of them compared to twelve girls. I also had my own room, and it was good to finally be able to stay in the home with the children at long last.

Chapter 12
The First Time in Our New Home

The infamous white helicopter that was far from safe had now ceased to operate, so instead, we had a water taxi. This was a small boat with an outboard motor that took about twelve people. If you were lucky, you could reach the other side in about an hour. It was at least a lot safer than the helicopter, although, at times, it was a bit rough.

Alan came out with me again in 2011 and we arrived at the home very late at night. It was wonderful to finally be able to see the children fast asleep in their new home and to sleep under the same roof as them. There was no electricity or generator, as the old one had died, so no lights or fans to cool us down from the now unbearable heat, and no running water either! Welcome to Africa, or as we said TIA – This Is Africa!

The next morning, I awoke to the sound of the children quietly getting ready to go to school! It was wonderful to finally wake up with them for the first time. I had my room upstairs which doubled as an office too. It had a spare bed in case any of the children were sick. Alan had Abi's room downstairs, which was a great improvement from the previous time!

I'd taken out some porridge oats to have for our breakfast, so I set about trying to make it. First light the fire to cook it on and that took at least an hour to get it hot. Then find a clean pan to put the water in and the porridge oats. It makes you realise how lucky we are in the UK to have electricity or gas to cook with. After around one hour, we eventually had hot porridge for breakfast!

Rosemary cooking her porridge

About two weeks before we flew out, Abi had found a little boy on the streets in town. He was about eight years old, and his name was Jonny. When we arrived he was sleeping on the floor in the little house where our security man lived with his wife and two children in our compound. He was very sick and withdrawn. His mother had recently drowned when a small, overloaded boat she was in, sank on its way to the Gambia. She had gone to buy cloth to sell and never came back.

Abi had been looking after him and paying for medicines with her own money. We brought him into the home, and he shared a bed with Hassan, one of our younger boys. Instead of getting better though, he got worse and had an abdominal obstruction. He needed to go to hospital urgently, so we took him and Aunty Hannah, one of our housemothers, so she could stay with little Jonny in hospital.

He needed blood, and we had to buy this from a man who was standing outside the hospital selling his blood! (I told you it was a different world out there!)

Jonny was in the hospital for quite a few days but eventually came out and I looked after him at home. Little by little, he became stronger and was able to play with the other children who had been wonderful with him.

We needed to take him to Social Welfare and to the police to see if anyone had reported him missing, as he had been taken from the streets. They had done the relevant paperwork and if no one claimed him, we would look after him.

It was lovely to see him interact with the other children, and they had taken him to their hearts as their brother. It was such a transformation from when he was first brought in.

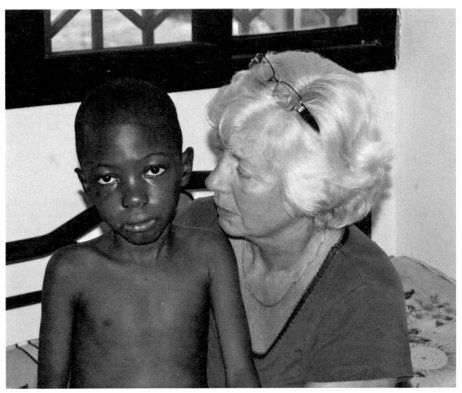
Jonny still very sick but back home with Grandma Rose to get well

We had employed a new manager when Alan and I were there the previous time and had left strict instructions for him **not** to use the 4x4. He didn't have a driving licence and showed no interest in it.

So, what a shock we had when we looked in the garage and saw our lovely Nissan 4x4! It wasn't quite as we had left it! Clearly, he had driven it, and someone said they had seen it in town!

It looked decidedly poorly with three flat tyres and a puncture. The battery also appeared to be flat. This was not a good start.

Unfortunately, they don't look after things as we do, and I think it's partly because they have not had to save up to buy things as we do.

I used to instill in the children that there was no need for them to ever steal. They had been given a new life and really appreciated that. I wanted them to be different.

We set about finding a mechanic, which took us four days. This meant that we couldn't do what we needed to do without a vehicle. Our home was up a very bad potholed road, and no taxis would ever come up, as they feared their vehicles would fall apart! As it was, they were usually held together by fresh air anyway!

Finally, we found one who could get our vehicle up and running, having parted with a large sum of money to get it fixed. We set off to go into town but hadn't gone far before we discovered we had another flat tyre! This was very frustrating as it took up valuable time. There is no such thing as the RAC or Green Flag! It was just left to us.

As time went by, we became aware of the poor state our 4x4 was in. We had to hand-start it every time we went anywhere, and it got to the stage where it struggled to go anywhere. Things were going from bad to worse with it and I was becoming increasingly concerned about being out there on my own and having to drive it. There was no way I could do what Alan was doing to get it going every time. It simply wasn't safe for me to drive.

Needless to say, the manager was dismissed!

Did you know that our British Forces were based in Sierra Leone, and you would often see them about town? I suddenly had a thought; I wonder what they did with their old vehicles? There was only one way to find out.

By chance, a few days later, we were in our vehicle behind one of theirs in a long line of standing traffic in town. What had I got to lose? I jumped out of our vehicle, ran up to theirs and tapped on the window! The officer jumped out of his skin and wasn't expecting to see a white woman at his window for sure! "Can I come in?" I said. "Yes, okay." He opened the passenger door and I climbed in as elegantly as I could, not realising how high up it was! "I'm very sorry to bother you, but I wonder if you could help me? My name is Rosemary Bidwell and I have an orphanage in Marjay Town, near Lumley beach, and we are desperately in need of a 4x4." He said they auctioned them off from time to time so there might be a chance of getting one of those. *Brilliant*, I thought! Well, if you don't ask, you don't get it!

He seemed quite taken with my question and gave me his business card to contact him via email. I thanked him kindly and tried very hard to clamber out as dignified as I could! This was going to be my next mission when I got home, but until then, we had to make the best of what we had and move on to deal with other pressing issues.

There was always something to be done and we had been having problems with the water. Some days, the water board would give us water and other days it would turn it off! Just like the electricity! The antiquated system couldn't cope with the demand, so the government would have to decide who had water and electricity and who wouldn't! Apart from the presidential home, of course, where they didn't have a problem at all!

Because our house had been left empty for a long time, the taps and pipes had seized up. We arranged to meet with a plumber and go over the whole house identifying the areas of concern. The plumber eventually came, but without his bag of tools, and all the jobs needed tools, so we ended up having to buy taps and spanners for him to do the job! All the workmen eventually come, never on time, often hours or days later, with no tools to do anything, which is so frustrating!

The girls' bedroom was a real concern as we had water pouring out from a leaking pipe under their sink and causing flooding on the floor which was an accident waiting to happen. It was simply not safe. Alan set about trying to fix it temporarily and in his words 'the house was leaking like a sieve with water pouring out everywhere!'

The health of the children was paramount and a particular concern this time as a number of the children were really sick. Some had malaria and three had typhoid as well, so we needed to get them extra medicines urgently.

Our other concern was that they didn't see dangers around the compound, some made by themselves! So Alan decided we needed to give them a health and safety talk. We lined them all up on the benches and Alan used the brick wall as a blackboard. We then got them to go around the compound and identify all the dangerous objects. This was a good exercise, as they had no idea of the danger that surrounded them.

Alan teaching the children and staff about health & safety

Chapter 13
Daily Life in Sierra Leone

Having returned from Freetown in February 2012, I had to accept that the vehicle had been completely ruined and was beyond economical repair. But for £500, it did us proud, thanks to Martin!

I realised that our next move was to start to raise money urgently in order to try and buy a vehicle from our British Forces in Sierra Leone called IMATT, which stands for International Military Assistance and Training Team. In their auction in April 2012. I began by putting posts on our Facebook page pleading for help. Donations soon started to come in from people far and wide, many of whom I had never met.

I made two short videos of our life in Africa and did presentations in churches. Come the day of the auction, we had raised exactly £4,000 in just less than ten weeks!

With a friend going to view the Land-Rover Defender vehicles for us in Sierra Leone and relaying the chassis numbers to us in the UK, we put in a bid on a vehicle with our £4,000. Unfortunately, we were way out, as it went for £10,000!

People had submitted multiple bids and therefore were disqualified, so another auction of ten remaining vehicles was held and we put in a bid for another vehicle. Sadly, this time we just missed by £200!

Now feeling disappointed, the guys at IMATT were also feeling sorry for us as they could see our desperate need for a vehicle. They had one last vehicle which they offered to us provided we could fly out and view it by the following Thursday. I hastily booked a flight and landed at 4 a.m., four days later on the day of the viewing. What we were met with was soul-destroying.

The vehicle had dented bodywork, split and torn seats, half the dashboard missing, and that was before we looked under the bonnet!

We agreed there was no way we could spend our sponsors' money on this and left in silence making our way back to the home to face telling the children.

Determined not to be beaten, I started to look around to see if there were any other suitable vehicles for sale.

Abi, now our manager, began calling her friends, and having trundled through back streets and alleyways to look at a vehicle we were told was for sale, I found a pickup truck with no number plate, holes in the floor and rust everywhere! This wasn't working out as I had hoped, and the prospect of getting a vehicle out there was now almost impossible.

Getting back to the daily routine, it soon became clear that Abi had got the housekeeping off to a fine art. She knew exactly how many sachets of dried milk would last a month, along with laundry soap, bags of rice, cassava leaves and other perishables.

I felt the staff would all benefit from having weekly meetings whilst I was out there. This would give them all the chance to discuss any concerns they would have.

A Typical Day.

Our day started at 5:30 a.m. with the sound of children scuttling around outside my bedroom door.

You'd hear the usual sounds of children getting dressed for school and chatting together tidying their bedrooms and making their beds.

I could hear someone sweeping with the hand brush made of palm twigs outside my bedroom door and sometimes if I went out to say 'good morning', they would say, "Grandma Rose, excuse, the sweeper is busy!'

Hassan with his 'sweeper'

Auntie Sarah checking their homework

This was followed by several knocks on the door. "Grandma, good morning, how you do?" They would say in broken English. They then went outside on the front steps to have their drink of warm milky tea and bread loaf for breakfast. They all had a role to play, and it was wonderful to see them busily getting ready for school. Sarah, our new manager, was often heard asking them where their school bags were, before checking they had all done their homework.

With singing and daily prayers, they would all hold hands on the front steps before they trooped off to school for 8 a.m. with haversacks on their backs, some nearly as big as they were!

They would all wave at me, followed by the now traditional blowing of a kiss and happy smiles. I felt extremely proud of every one of them, and so happy to be living there with them.

I felt so at home with them all and felt I belonged. So much so that I even shipped out my mother's old round coffee table to have in my room. A little bit of home and history.

After the children had left for school, the aunties began to do all the washing. This was done on an old washboard bending over a large bowl of cold water and with a small bar of laundry soap. It was then hung up on seven washing lines to dry!

Daily washing

The preparation of food was very time consuming, chopping the leaves and onions and pounding the peppers with the daily fifteen cups of rice!

Fish was very expensive, so they had been eating more leaves. These were cooked in our outside kitchen on an open fire in pots called 'Wonder Pots'.

This was a good name for them as I often 'wondered' what went into these pots!

Preparing the food

The younger children came home at 12:30 p.m. and the older ones at 2 p.m. The two older boys, Augustine and Momoh, had a very long walk of well over an hour to get to their school, but it was a good school, so they didn't mind.

They would all change out of their uniforms and wash them themselves, along with their shoes, as they got so dusty. The two youngest little boys, Alimamy and Ibrahim, were still too young to do their washing but helped the aunties to wash their shoes and left them in the sun to dry.

When all the children were back, they would sit at the two tables indoors and have their meal. After they'd finished, they would take their bowls and wash them up, saying, "Grandma Rose, thank you," as they went.

Mealtime at the table for the young ones

The heat and humidity was something else. As they had been up since 5:30 a.m. they were all very tired, so they all went to their beds to sleep.

When they woke up, they would all do their homework. Once this was completed, it was time to play. They would amuse themselves with anything but really loved it when we went out into the compound and played games with them.

They loved to come and sit with me on the veranda. This was a very precious time. Every child needs to be loved and feel loved, so with all these children to care for, this was quite hard sometimes for the housemothers to give them individual attention. It was a unique opportunity for me to get to know them more.

When I brought them in, they were all so traumatised and I guess I will never really know what they had been through.

One little girl didn't smile for three years, now, she always smiles.

They have all come a long way from when I rescued them seven years ago. They know now that they are safe and very much loved.

The girls love to plait their hair, so I bought them all Barbie Dolls for them to play with! They thought this was wonderful!

The boys loved to play football in the compound and would do it bare-footed. We also flew out two old tennis rackets and some tennis balls and the older boys loved to play with them. We used an old bench for the net and sometimes the younger children sat on it but that didn't seem to bother them playing!

It was dark by 7:30 p.m., so at 6:30 p.m. they would have 'Pap', which was like semolina, and milky tea or cocoa before doing our singing and thanking God before going to bed.

N'Mah cooking tea called 'Pap' (like semolina) in the outside kitchen

Everyone was in bed by 9 p.m., including me. Sleeping in the relentless heat was so hard. With the mosquito mesh at the open windows, I tried to sleep with the sounds of barking dogs fighting in the surrounding area and general noise.

After the children were in bed, I would sit on my veranda and reflect on the day's events and our achievements. I would often lay on the spare mattress on the veranda and listen to the night sounds of children crying outside in the neighbouring area along with the noise of loud frogs and other wildlife, looking up at the moon and the stars.

This was my West African home and I loved it!

I was reminded of God's wonder, as it's the same moon all over the world. I would tell the children that when they felt sad and afraid at night, they were to look up to the moon, put their finger on it and know that it was the same moon I would see in England. We could do the same and feel the love and closeness it brought.

Sometimes, I would fall asleep on the mattress outside but would wake up about 3 a.m. and go and lie on my bed for the rest of the night.

When I went out in May or June, it would be especially hot and humid as it was the start of the rainy season. I would sit on my veranda and see the lightning over the green mountains in the distance. I knew it was going to be a long night with very strong winds and heavy rains as the thunderstorms got closer.

In 1462, the region which became the country of Sierra Leone was visited by the Portuguese explorer named Pedro da Cintra who dubbed it Sierra de Leao, meaning 'lion mountains'. This is where the name Sierra Leone comes from, mountain lion.

Our damp ceilings

The rains would lash against the windows, and as the buildings were not well built the rains would come through the roof and flood my bedroom floor.

Augustine, our eldest boy, had to move his bed, as the roof was leaking above him. It was the same in the housemothers' bedroom.

We had recently been given a generator, which hopefully would mean we would have powered a bit more. We then needed the fuel to put in it, so Momoh, our second eldest boy, would walk three miles to get it!

Everything here was a struggle, but this would bring light into the home so the children could do their reading and homework at nighttime.

As a special treat at the weekend, they would watch the television someone donated, but it only played DVDs. They showed me what they had been watching which was a very poor copy of an old Indian film, which they seem to love. I guess when there's nothing else to watch, anything will do!

I decided to get some videos from a charity shop and take them out. I bought children's films and cartoons, including Mr Bean! I thought they would understand the humour!

With the new generator, I decided to buy a freezer. Something we take for granted in the UK but if you imagine our summer heat and treble it without a freezer, that's how hard it is.

It would mean that the food they bought daily could be kept in the freezer. This meant they didn't have to cook the meat and fish the same day they bought it and leave it upstairs in their bedroom until they needed it in the week, which was not good as it attracted the flies!

I must emphasise that we did not have power every day. We had to wait for the government to decide if it was our day for electricity, and if not, then we put our generator on for about two hours every evening. This would be particularly useful now as we started the rainy season. Our road very quickly turned into a fast-flooding river, and we simply couldn't get up or down the roads to get provisions.

As the girls were now becoming older, they were showing signs of wanting to do more creative activities. Auntie Christiana, one of the housemothers, could make soap, so in the children's holidays in July, she taught them how to make it.

We also shipped out an old Singer treadle sewing machine and I taught them how to sew and mend their clothes. Tailoring was a good job to have out there and very important, as so many people needed clothes made for them.

People would set up a little business on the side of the street and sew.

We were also given some old white quilt covers that had seen better days, so we decided to unpick them and halve the quilt covers, making two sheets to dye in different colours so they would look nice on the children's beds.

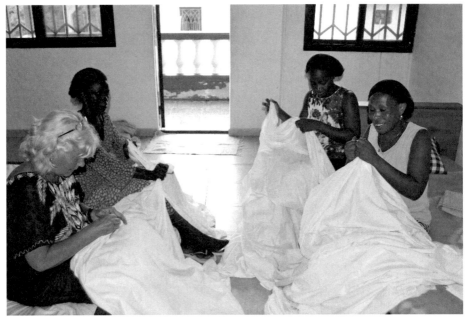

Separating the quilt covers to make sheets to dye

Three of our children celebrated their birthdays whilst I was there, so I asked them what they wanted. "A pair of shoes for school, a school bag and some biscuits please!" Wouldn't it be wonderful if our English children were so easily pleased!

On their birthdays, we all walked to the street stall down our road, and they chose what soft drinks and biscuits they wanted. We also bought mangos and oranges as a special treat!

Without our vehicle, we were stuck and couldn't go anywhere, but I did manage to hire a vehicle to take them to the beach in.

I took the older ones for a walk along the beach, and we found some beautiful shells. The girls were wearing sort of hairnets at the time to protect their hair from getting wet, so we put all the shells in their hairnets and took them back to play with on the beach. When we got back home, they were so fascinated with them we decided to make a hole in them to thread some ribbon to make necklaces!

Alimatu ironing her school uniform

Alimatu, our oldest girl of fifteen, came home from school one day with a letter saying she had to write an essay to be chosen to go on a young girls camp for a day. A bit like the Girl Guides. She had to write an essay on why she thought she should be chosen.

Their mission statement was to 'empower, to inspire and enlighten others'.

First, we got her dictionary out to look up the three words so she would understand their meaning. They were so hungry to learn and remembered everything they were taught.

Then we set about putting this in an essay and why she believed she should be chosen.

This was a big thing for Alimatu. She had gone from having nothing and no hope of ever having anything, to being able to go to school, having regular food to eat and having her own bed. Now she was writing about why she thought she deserved to go to this camp!

Off she went to school the next day with a beaming smile on her face. I loved spending quality time with her. These are the things we naturally do as parents for our children, but for them, it's simply a matter of survival.

When she came home we were all outside playing. "Grandma, I have been chosen to go," she said. This was absolutely amazing! We all cheered, and the children jumped with joy! We were so thrilled with her achievement and everyone learnt from Alimatu's three core words of: empower, inspire and enlighten others.

Sitting on the back steps having fun at supper time

Our English visitors

I had to go into town one day to change some money, and on the way back, Abi and I stopped for a drink. Also having a drink were two English ladies. Abi said she knew them. It turned out that one of them had been to the home in January! They had come to give training at a local hospital, and they were so taken with our children in January that they wanted to visit us again.

They asked how the charity was started and on the journey, back in the taxi I began to tell 'Our Story of Hope and Happiness'. Tears filled their eyes, and they were visibly moved.

We arrived home and were all greeted by the children nearly knocking us over, giving lots of hugs. This was their way of saying how much they appreciated us. The children were fascinated with one lady's sun hat and began trying it on!

We all sat outside on our benches and the children wanted to do their special welcome presentation for our two guests, Pat, and Julie. They only stayed for a couple of hours, but they left feeling truly blessed, just as we did from their visit.

Sunday was the day when they all got dressed up in their Sunday best and went to the local church. The older girls were now very aware of how they looked and came down from their bedrooms looking very smart. They loved having their photo taken and enjoyed posing on the steps of our home in their best clothes. One girl, Nancy, would often go back to change two or three times before she was ready, so I used to call her 'Fancy Nancy'!

After lunch and a rest, they would do their letter writing to their sponsors. You have no idea how important their sponsors were to them! They truly were their lifelines.

If it were not for them, they would not be able to go to school and have a future. They loved receiving letters from their sponsors too, and it was always the first thing they would say when I arrived, "Grandma Rose, how is my sponsor?"

Their Health

They were only ever a breath away from becoming sick with either malaria, or typhoid, or even worse.

One day, I noticed one of the girls, who was eleven, limping. She had tripped over and cut her toe. After a few days, it became increasingly painful and swollen until I noticed, she was looking very sick and sleeping a lot over the weekend.

When I looked again, her toe was now very infected. It's almost impossible to keep everything clean due to the dust and filthy conditions. I decided she needed to go to the hospital but as we had no vehicle this was a problem. She couldn't walk on it all the way down the road, so we called a friend who had a motorbike, and he took her to the hospital. They decided it was so infected that she had to have her nail removed. What a brave girl she was! With no aid of local anaesthetic available, it was excruciating for her!

She came home with antibiotics and lay resting to recover.

Children are very brave out there and never make a fuss about anything!

The day had come for me to return home to the UK.

Rosie, who was now nine, had been bitten on her leg by a stray dog while walking back to the home. This was so dangerous because of rabies. Abi had to take her to the hospital to be injected and the wound dressed. This was not a good time to be going back to the UK, but then there never would be a good time.

I always had an open flight ticket, so I used to stay as long as possible to try and accomplish everything I had set out to do.

I couldn't put it off any longer. It was time to return home.

I was up early once again with the children, but this time it was to pack my suitcase to catch my flight. All the children came knocking on my door to be with me while I packed. They never wanted me to go. Rosie even got into my suitcase and said, "Please take me with you, Grandma."

Somehow, I needed to get to the water taxi that would take me to the airport. Once again, Abi managed to arrange this. She called her friend who was a driver at the local hospital where we took our children and begged him to take me. He arrived in a vehicle very similar to the one we had come out to buy, and as I put my cases in it, I couldn't help feeling sad.

Fighting back the tears, I got all the children to line up so I could give each one a farewell hug and a kiss.

They all stood silently with tears running down their faces as I waved them goodbye.

Chapter 14
Fundraising in the UK

After the long journey home, I awoke the next morning and looked out of my window. Everywhere was silent but I could still hear the sound of my lovely children ringing in my ears. Everywhere was so clean and green. Such a contrast to the backdrop of the red dusty roads, the familiar noises and smells of Africa and the daily struggle in a country that children didn't ask to be born into and had no choice but to survive.

I would go out to Sierra Leone every two to three months, or whenever there was an emergency.

During my time in the UK, I would spend my time fund-raising and giving presentations to organisations, schools, and churches. They were always fascinated to see the development of the children and see the difference in how they had grown. We always needed more sponsors, so part of my presentations was to encourage new sponsorship.

The Boys Brigade at Leamington Spa Baptist church presented me with this wonderful picture and donation of coins in the form of 'The Cotton Tree Children's Trust'!

Committee members ran car boot sales and even sold other items to raise funds.

One of the things we organised every year was a charity cake sale and presentation at a local school in Warwickshire.

They used to open up their school every Sunday afternoon from March to October and different charities would provide afternoon tea and cakes to raise money for their chosen charity.

We did this for over six years and had become well known in the area. I put together a display in the hall where the teas and cakes were sold, and as people came through, they could see the work we were doing.

We usually held this on a Sunday in June and the weather was often sunny, so we were able to have the picnic benches outside too.

People came from miles around for bike rides or just country walks as the venue was set in the lovely Warwickshire countryside.

I used to makeover twenty large cakes of all different flavours along with scones and cream and jam, which were always a hit! This was no effort for me, as I loved baking!

A team of volunteers and committee members helped and my friend Annie, who I'd known for a number of years, was brilliant in the kitchen with the dishwasher! I called her our kitchen queen!

We served teas and coffees to go with a slice of homemade cake or scone. It was great fun and we all enjoyed doing it each year to raise much-needed funds.

Another event, at Christmas, was an auction evening with music and a buffet. This also raised a lot of money. As the saying goes…'Every little helps!' And in Sierra Leone, it goes a very long way!

Some people think it's hard to fundraise, but I firmly believe that if you are passionate enough about your cause, people will buy into it. If I found a penny on the ground, I would enter it into our accounts.

One such occasion was on a BMI flight out to Freetown when I always used to wear my 'Cotton Tree Children's Trust' T-shirt so people could see what we were doing in Sierra Leone.

One of the air stewardesses happened to comment on it and wanted to know more. She was so taken that she and her crew asked if they could visit our home when we landed as they were staying over for three days until the next flight back.

I gave them directions and they all came up to see us! They were completely overwhelmed to see what we were doing – and by an English charity too!

They had been more used to hearing people on the plane who represented global charities, discussing how they were going to spend their time, and on which beach to meet once they had finished their work!

The BMI crew all decided they wanted to help more so after our usual welcome songs to them all, they left with tears of emotion.

Soon after, I had a call from one of them to say they had put the word out to their colleagues and had collected four suitcases full of shoes, clothes, and toothbrushes, as well as sweets for the children. They flew these out the next time they were there, to take to our home!

One of them did the Three Peaks Challenge whilst in the UK and raised over £1,000 for us!

They were amazing and would often return to see our children when they were in Freetown on a stop-over, including one occasion when they arranged to take all our children to the beach for a treat!

When I brought Abi and Rosie to the UK in 2006, the local media got to hear about their visit and wanted to do an article on us all.

I was then contacted by BBC Midlands Today who came out to do a piece on the girls. This went out on the six o'clock news, and it wasn't long before I was inundated with calls from people as far away as Wales wanting to help, donate and sponsor the children. One lovely lady decided to knit them all a teddy, which was lovely, as they hadn't any toys of their own. She made us one hundred teddies to sell at a Christmas stall for £1 each to raise even more money for the children!

The other thing I desperately needed to do was to try and find us a vehicle. Another member of our committee worked for Jaguar Land Rover in Coventry and knew more about cars than I did, so he set about trying to find us one.

We had already raised £4,000, so this was a good start. He came across a Freelander that was in fairly good condition, so we agreed to buy it and he took it into his workshop at JLR (Jaguar Land Rover) where all the guys volunteered to do all the maintenance and repairs for us in their spare time for free!

They enjoyed doing this for us and by the time they had finished, it looked like a new vehicle, including having our own 'Cotton Tree Children's Trust' sign on the side!

Since my last visit to Sierra Leone, they had changed the law and all vehicles shipped out had to be left-hand drive. Our old one was a right-hand drive and I got quite used to driving on the left with a right-hand drive vehicle!

This meant that our new Freelander had to be converted to a left-hand drive. We found a place in London that could do it for us, and I drove the Freelander down to London to find it! I had to leave the vehicle there for the job to be done, and then I went back down to see it.

As any mechanic would know, it's not the easiest thing to do but they managed it. I then proceeded to drive it back as a left-hand vehicle!

Looking back, I'd done some crazy things, and this was one of them! Now we had our vehicle, it was time to pack it full of things for the children.

A private school had donated all their summer school uniforms, and our sponsors had all donated money for me to buy the children a scooter each for the children. Argos must have wondered what on earth I was doing buying twenty scooters!

All these presents and many other things for the children were packed into the vehicle ready to be shipped out, but this time, in a sealed container!

I drove down to London once again to the shipping company and watched tentatively as they loaded our precious cargo into the container.

That was it; I could do no more than prepare to fly out to clear the vehicle in Freetown!

Chapter 15
Assaulted and Abused

I shipped our second-hand Freelander 4x4 out to Freetown in November 2013. There it was put into a container, locked, and sealed for its long journey to Freetown.

My plan was to fly out just before it docked so I could complete all the paperwork to clear it, but as we know, things don't always go according to plan, especially in Freetown! As we say TIA – This Is Africa!

I flew out to begin the long and difficult challenge ahead.

On arrival, I was again greeted by our lovely children, who were thrilled to see me and excited that we would all be celebrating Christmas altogether.

I contacted the shipping company but there was no definite news of the ship docking, other than 'it shouldn't be much longer'.

Still, without a vehicle, I had to concentrate on the things I could do. One was to visit the children's school, but first I needed to spend time with the housemothers and get up to date on what had been happening within the home.

Once this was done, I could go up to the school, but before I got that far, the children came running home saying the headmaster wanted to see me. This didn't surprise me, as I knew it would be an excuse to try and get money.

This went on for a few days until one day, they came home saying only half their school fees had been paid. This couldn't be right, as I knew I had paid them.

The next day, they came home with a letter and an envelope attached to give to me. The letter was from their headmaster asking the children to pay money for his wedding! I couldn't quite believe it. I wrote back saying, "Thank you for your letter, but as an orphanage, we are not in a position to give any more money as we have twenty children to feed and care for, but we hope you have a lovely day!"

The next day, the children went off to school, as usual, taking my letter with them. Halfway through the morning, some of the children returned home! I was working in the compound, and they said the headmaster had sent them home! "Why?" I asked. They said it was because I hadn't paid their school fees! Something was definitely not right. I dropped what I was doing and walked over a mile up to their school to see what was going on. I was met halfway by the rest of the children coming home, as they too had been sent home.

I arrived at the school and was met by an aggressive headmaster. We sat down in his office, and he began by saying I had only paid half the school fees and I needed to pay the rest. I insisted that I had sent the full amount and was not prepared to give any more. This was no small amount either; it was for a whole term's fee for sixteen of our children!

Whilst I was there, I asked him about the letter he had sent home asking for money to pay for his wedding. At this point, he could not contain himself any longer and went into a fit of temper, shouting at me very loudly as he realised he should not have done that!

He then shouted for his staff to come quickly and immediately they came running. They held me back and prevented me from leaving the school building and wouldn't stop shouting at me.

It was quite unbelievable what they were doing. I stood in the middle of all this chaos with the women teachers shouting across each other and physically grabbing me by the arms to prevent me from leaving, drawing blood. In the end, I shouted as loud as I knew how to, "Let me go."

After many minutes, I managed to break free and force my way through them to get out of the building and hurried from the school compound. They all quickly followed, still shouting abuse at me, saying, "Go back to your country. We don't want you here."

I hurried home with blood pouring down my arms. By the time I reached home, I was in an awful state. The housemothers were horrified to see what had happened to me and said I needed to inform the police, but I still didn't have a vehicle.

I had friends called Femi and Mabinty who owned a hotel in Freetown, so I walked down the long track to the main road, still bleeding to try and get a taxi to take me into town. As per usual, this took over two hours, so by the time I arrived, I had flies crawling all over my arms where I was bleeding.

The police were informed, and I was sent to the hospital to have my arms dressed before they became infected. I was also told I had to report the incident to the British Embassy who was equally as horrified to see what had happened, 'especially to a white woman who had gone out to do humanitarian work'. They had to then write a report and send it to Whitehall in London.

I had to do the return journey back to the home, which took another few hours. This whole episode took all day! I sat on my bed and questioned why on earth had I put myself through all of this.

I had set out to rescue these dear children and give them a better life, yet there were many times this was lost on obstructive adults who simply saw me as 'the white woman' they didn't respect.

During all my visits, I kept a daily diary, which I found invaluable and very therapeutic. On many of my trips, I travelled alone, and it was so hard at times not to have anyone to share things with.

The headmaster refused to accept the children back, so they had to stay at home and we all home schooled them. I was not prepared to be treated this way and was certainly not giving in to his demands. I knew exactly what he was trying to do, and he underestimated my knowledge of his country.

Chapter 16
Frustrations Galore!

Once I had recovered from the ordeal at school, I had to get back to the issue of clearing our vehicle.

We had word that the ship had finally docked and in a few days, we would be able to get out the vehicle. Or so I thought!

Abi came to help me as we were passed from one office to another. You'd go to one office, only to be told that you needed to go to another one first, and when you got there, you were told it was the wrong office and you needed to go elsewhere!

This happened day after day after day and became very frustrating. The forms we had to fill in were equally as difficult and frustrating and nobody seemed to know what was supposed to be happening! It was as if they'd never done this process of clearing a vehicle before and had no idea!

I had to send Abi into the offices and stay well-hidden so they couldn't see me, otherwise, we would have been charged at least double the price. Even Abi said, on one occasion, "Mum, even though we are black, we trust no one!"

Abi could see I was getting physically weaker and said, "Don't worry, I'll take over from here."

Each day, I would come home exhausted having achieved nothing. I recall writing in my diary that I had only eaten a cereal bar that day, and nothing else.

I used to go without proper food for up to three days, and then I would buy food when I was next in town. There were no shops near the home to buy food.

By the end of an exhausting day with temperatures around 30-40 degrees, I just wanted to go to sleep. I was beyond hungry.

I would call it the SL Diet as I would lose about a stone in weight!

On one occasion, we were sent to the Minister of Finance on the eighth floor with no lifts, to add our signature to papers for the release of our vehicle, but when we got there, the minister was blind and couldn't see that his boss had not yet signed it! We had to tell him. His boss had just left for South Africa that day and would be gone for weeks and had forgotten to sign it before he left. The blind minister, of course, couldn't see this! T.I.A! This is Africa!

This, if you recall is the Christmas period, so everywhere we went we had to pay 'Christmas Tips'.

I remember seeing a woman, all dressed up with false eyelashes, begging on the street. She, along with hundreds of others were asking me to give them money for Christmas. I couldn't help thinking to myself, *how about they give me some of their money to help the children in their own country!*

All I seemed to be doing was giving out money upon money to clear this vehicle.

After weeks of utter frustration, I decided to go down to the docks myself very early one morning and try to get our vehicle out. I set off at 5:30 a.m. and walked down the long potholed road to the main road to see if I could get a taxi to take me to the docks. I managed to do this and arrived at the docks at 10:30 a.m.

I presented myself at numerous offices, again being shunted from pillar to post and refusing to move until I had answers.

Hours went by and the heat got hotter, but still, I refused to leave without our vehicle.

Eventually, at 3:00 p.m., someone said, "Ma, your vehicle is up there in that top container." I raised my eyes to see, but it was stacked behind other large containers, which had to be moved first.

Another hour went by, and another, until a man eventually decided to bring his large forklift truck and begin to move the other containers in front of ours. Just as I thought we were getting somewhere, he stopped working and drove off! Now what! He had apparently been called to do something else.

Sadly, as a woman, even more, as a white woman, you are given little or no respect. You just have to fight to be heard.

I sat down on a large block of concrete trying to find some shade and not allowing them to see my frustration.

Another hour went by until I had to eventually ask someone what was happening. After another hour the same man came back and continued moving the containers to get to ours. By now it was 5 p.m. and some of the offices were closing!

Then finally it was time for ours to come down. At last!

Once on the ground, I needed to check it and get papers signed off, but the offices were now closed. I was told to come back the next day, but I wasn't going to leave, as I knew it was a ploy to get more money out of me for keeping our container another day on the docks. I was already being charged a daily rate for having it there.

I managed to find someone who would sign my papers, at a cost, of course! Eventually, we got the cutters to cut the seal so we could open the doors. Everything was still intact, and the man reversed it out of the container. Hooray! At long last, I could drive our vehicle, but before I could drive home, I needed to get petrol. One of the men offered to fill it up at the dock, so I gave him the money and off he went.

By this time, it was pitch black and I couldn't see a thing.

He soon returned with the vehicle and disappeared. I was now left to find my way out of the docks and onto the narrow road, which would eventually lead me to the main road.

As I was driving, I suddenly looked down at the petrol gauge, only to see that the man had not put any petrol in at all but had just taken my money! So I had to try and find a petrol station that had petrol to sell. Out there, you can go to as many as five petrol stations before you find petrol! They sell out!

I managed to find my way home in the dark. I turned into our unmade road full of potholes eighteen hours later; I could hear the children waiting excitedly in the night air for me to return with our new vehicle!

The next morning, they were all eager to see our new second-hand vehicle and sang songs of joy and clapped their hands!

I suddenly caught sight of one little boy called Ibrahim, looking at himself in the wing mirror! His face was a picture! He had never seen himself before and couldn't quite work out what he was seeing! I had to explain that the lovely little boy looking at him in the mirror was him!

This would now make a huge difference for me to get around and do my work. As it was Christmas, everything was closed so we had to wait until after New Year before I could get our Sierra Leone number plates.

The police were very hot on this, especially at Christmas, as they would find any excuse to stop you in order to get money off you for their Christmas box! Once again, I was the wrong combination of being a white woman and kept getting stopped because of the UK number plates, despite having the correct documents. I still had to pay them before they would let me go!

Amongst other things, I had shipped out all their scooters for Christmas, so on Christmas Eve, Abi and I sat up into the early hours, putting them all together for the morning.

Christmas day had finally come. The day started like any other day with the children knocking on my bedroom door at 5:30 a.m. wanting me to open it so they could say, "Grandma Rose, good morning," followed by a big hug.

We all went downstairs, and their faces were a picture! They just couldn't believe what they saw! What on earth were these things Grandma had brought from their sponsors?

I had to show them what they were, which was a laugh in itself. Then, one by one, they took their scooters outside and began to try and ride them!

What I hadn't taken into account was the number of plasters I would need as they constantly fell off, but never did they shed one tear! Just perseverance to master this peculiar pastime.

Even the housemothers wanted a go, and we all fell about laughing!

This was how it should be for these children. They have to grow up so quickly and don't have a childhood.

After all this excitement, it was time for them to have breakfast and get into their Sunday best outfits ready to go to church. Off they went whilst the housemothers and I prepared their dinner outside – chopping, grinding, and cooking their Christmas dinner. No turkey for them, or stuffing, or any other trimmings. But to them, this was luxury with special rice. No Christmas pudding either, as they don't have any desserts, but I had bought some bananas and oranges which they loved.

As they all sat on their benches outside, quietly appreciating their special Christmas dinner, I was sat on a large, covered drain as my thoughts turned to home and people's plates piled high with far too much food they didn't need.

My friend had given me a mince pie to take out, which by now, was well and truly squashed, as it hadn't travelled well. This was my Christmas dinner! As I sat on the drain, I took a very small bite and savoured every bit of it, for this squashed mince pie **was** my Christmas dinner. It was all I had!

I sat thinking about friends at home and compared the vast differences. On that large drain with my squashed mince pie, I was nearer to the real meaning of

Christmas. This was my home now. There is a sign in Sierra Leone, which says, 'There is no success without a struggle.' This was so true.

We had all been invited to someone's house for tea, so at 4 p.m., we all got washed and changed and the children put on their charity 'Cotton Tree Children's Trust' T-shirts. It was hot and dusty as we all walked across the rough ground to where we had been invited.

The man whose home we were visiting worked for a bank in town. He had heard about us and the work we were doing, so he and his wife decided they wanted to say thank you by welcoming us all into their home. There are some very appreciative people in Freetown, which was lovely.

There was music for the children to dance to, and food and drink for everyone. I was introduced to members of his family, including one cousin who had flown in from Canada where he was now living. During the conversation, I asked him what took him to Canada, and he replied, "An aeroplane!" Well, I did ask!

After much merriment and a good few hours, it was time to make our way home. The children had had a brilliant time, and thoroughly spoilt.

Soon it was time for bed, so after our usual songs of happiness and thankfulness, they all picked up their scooters and put them at the bottom of their beds for the morning. They didn't look quite so shiny as they did but had given them so much fun and allowed them to be happy children on Christmas Day.

Boxing Day was like any other. The children were back to normal, carrying buckets of water on their heads to do all the lines of washing and helping prepare food as usual.

Now that we had the vehicle, I decided that they deserved their trip to the beach. I think I counted eleven children in the 4x4, and a friend came with an open-backed truck, which the older children went in. I loved our times at the beach. They were so precious.

The children sang some of their favourite songs as we drove along, and I felt I had finally achieved recognition in Freetown with our new logo on the side. I was forever counting all their heads just to make sure they were all there, but sometimes we ended up with more than we started as the beach children who were living rough used to join us and have fun too.

All going to the beach in our 4x4

Having fun in the sea

All sitting on the back steps Christmas 2013

Before I left England, a young girl heard about us and managed to get her school to donate all the girls' old summer uniforms! And here they are!

And our girls wearing them

Thank you for all our new shoes

Children with their scooters

Playing musical chairs

Playing in the banana trees

And cleaning our new 4x4

Our younger boys in the donated blazers

Collecting our water for the day

Chapter 17
To Hell and Back

This is probably the hardest chapter to write, and you will see why at the end.

After all the celebrations of Christmas, I was hoping to be able to get back to the work I was out there to do, but before I could get started, I had a call from the police saying they had the headmaster and two staff members in their office, and I was to attend a court meeting at the police station as the headmaster and staff wanted to bring a case against me just as things were getting back to normal, whatever normal was!

The next day, I got myself to the police station. I was put before the police commissioner who was clearly on the side of the headmaster and not in the least bit interested in what happened. I had to listen to the headmaster's lies and accusations.

Here I was giving up everything to make a difference to these innocent children's lives, at the cost of being wrongly accused of something I hadn't done!

A few days later, I was told that the headmaster had bribed the police and deliberately brought the case to court, as he knew he was in the wrong for stealing half the children's school fees and sending the letter home asking for money for his wedding. Another police department contacted me a while later to say they were investigating his actions and he had been suspended from school indefinitely!

As if this wasn't bad enough, I came back to the home to discover that one of the staff had been stealing bags of rice, dried milk, and sugar, taking it out of the home and giving it to a friend to store in order to sell.

This was serious. In all my years in Sierra Leone, I had never had to deal with a situation like this one.

One of the housemothers came to see me and I encouraged her to trust me. She eventually opened up and sure enough, we caught the member of staff in the act of handing over large bags of rice to her friend to store.

I decided to delve a bit deeper and found other food stored in her room ready to be sold. This was one step too far and as the person in question refused to tell the truth, I gave her an ultimatum: to return all the stolen food or she would be asked to leave.

She refused to return the goods and after three days, I deeply regretted having to write her a letter of dismissal. I asked for the keys to her room. Again, she was defiant and refused to leave. She went out locking her door behind her. We had no idea where she was and couldn't get inside her room.

I then had a call from the police asking me to attend the police station, as she had gone to them bribing them to have me arrested. I was being accused of stealing her money and her belongings. I couldn't believe what was happening to me. This was surely the worst trip I had ever had?

The next day, as summoned, I went to the police station and took a friend for support. The housemother who had done this was already there.

I was taken into a room and sat before a police officer who began to question me and write a statement on a sheet of plain paper with a pencil.

The two police officers wrote out statements in their own words, refusing to listen to what I was saying. I had to ask them to redo it over and over again as it was so inaccurate. Each time they introduced a new twist and at no time was this statement ever correct.

Whatever I said wasn't acceptable. I insisted he rubs it out and corrects it. He kept saying I was to sign it as a true record of what happened, and I kept refusing. Why would I sign something that wasn't true? This went on for hours on end.

I had arrived at 10 a.m. and by now, it was getting late. I had now been interrogated for eleven hours with nothing to eat or drink and had nothing left to give. After this traumatic ordeal, I couldn't take the strain any longer.

I was given the choice of signing the statement and going free or refusing and being charged. The pressure finally got too much for me and I broke down outside with chest pains. I sat on a wall completely distraught and in total disbelief.

These people were capable of the unbelievable!

My friends were equally shocked and horrified at what was happening and said it was nothing short of evil.

As I sat on the wall outside, the chest pains increased and became very concerning, so my friends decided I had to be taken to hospital. But the police refused to let me go.

My friends made a phone call to find someone who would act as bail for me, and then I was taken to hospital, but not as we know it! I lay on an old rusting bed with no sheets, just a dirty plastic mattress. The nurses were abrupt and uncaring. They tried to take blood samples but couldn't find a vein. After many hours, I had to be admitted for a suspected heart attack.

My friends contacted my insurance company and made them aware of the severity of the situation, as the hospital refused to cooperate.

I was asked what sort of ward I was prepared to pay for, one with no fans, or one with fans! I chose the one with fans.

This was awful as a hospital. There was mesh at the windows to stop the mosquitos, but it was broken, so here was I, in hospital with the very real added risk of catching malaria again!

I had no food or drink, so was dependent on friends bringing some in. Even the lady from the British Embassy had heard about what had happened and came to visit me bringing a packet of biscuits. She was horrified at what had happened.

Every few hours, they would come around to take more blood. This was to get more money from me!

Unbeknown to me, my insurance company had been in touch with the hospital frantically trying to establish what was happening. The doctor looking after me said I was refusing to co-operate and wouldn't allow him to take my blood!

Eventually, the insurance company insisted on speaking to me, to establish what was actually happening, and were shocked to hear how the doctor had lied in order to keep me in the hospital longer to get more money.

The insurance company were now very anxious and made the decision to airlift me out to a hospital in another country where I could receive proper medical attention.

I was put into an ambulance on a stretcher and driven by two porters along potholed roads down to the dock where I was lowered into a wooden boat and met by a member of the British Embassy who was to accompany me. Thank goodness nothing happened to me along the way, as I was the only person in that ambulance who knew what to do!

As I lay in the bottom of the boat, I looked up at the moon and stars and was totally at peace with whatever was to happen. Halfway across the water, in pitch darkness, the engine of the boat stalled and cut out. There was nothing I could do but lay there. Eventually, after about twenty minutes, he got it going again and we continued across the sea in the dug-out boat.

When we reached the other side, there waiting for me was a medical Cessna plane that had been flown in from Senegal to Sierra Leone with two doctors on board. I was put on the plane on a stretcher, and we took off for the five-hour flight to a hospital in Tenerife.

This particular night, there was a huge storm, and as I lay there, I could see the moon and stars darting across the sky. It was also very cold and there were no blankets. I just had to give in; I had nothing left to fight with.

Sierra Leone had taken everything I had.

As we approached the landing pad at the hospital, the weather conditions worsened, and the pilot had to land the Cessna in 100 mph gale force winds! My drip came off its stand, my oxygen cylinder was rolling along the floor of the plane, and we were being tossed around like pieces of paper.

Eventually, we landed on the helipad at the hospital, and I was taken by ambulance to the emergency department.

I was so scared as I was in a foreign hospital with absolutely nobody else I knew around me, and I couldn't understand what they were saying.

After being admitted to intensive care, I was taken to theatre and given an angiogram with the possibility of having a stent put in. I remained in hospital until I was strong enough to be flown home but very weak and traumatised.

Everything had been taken out of my hands. I hadn't even been able to say farewell to my lovely children. I wasn't even able to give them a last hug before I left.

I was sad, as I wasn't strong enough to endure what I had been put through. I felt I had let the children down badly and had no idea if or when I would ever see or hear from them again.

All my belongings were put into suitcases and flown back to me in the UK.

Social Welfare contacted me saying, they had heard that I had fled the country and abandoned all the children, and they would all have to be separated and go into care! Nothing was further from the truth!

I had now hit rock bottom and broke down in tears. After all I had done and fought for, I couldn't allow these dear children to be taken away. They were one big happy family. I had to think quickly, and I put one of the housemothers in charge so Social Welfare couldn't take them away.

It took a long while for me to recover from the ordeal, and I now realised I wasn't as strong as I thought I was. The stress of doing so much was becoming too great.

I had to take a big step back and look for a new vision for their future.

Chapter 18
Where to Now?

Word had got around of what had happened. People began to offer support and eventually wanted to serve on the committee. They could see I needed help, and this was exactly what I wanted to hear. I was looking forward to having more support.

One member's ten-year-old son decided to raise money by going on all the London underground tube trains in a particular order in a set time! He was amazing and raised a lot of money for us.

Another member's young daughter called Tamzin decided to walk a mile a day for the whole of December, including Christmas Day, and also raised a huge amount. Other events took place too.

It was at this time that I met a wonderful man named Ron. He had worked extensively throughout Africa during his career as a wildlife journalist and photographer, so we had a common interest in Africa. His wife of forty years had died some two years earlier.

We became good friends, fell in love and two years later, he proposed, and we got married.

Ron became our committee secretary and publicity officer and, in these capacities, provided me with invaluable support with what was to follow.

With everything that had happened, I decided I had to look for another orphanage that would offer us support, so using all my contacts, I managed to find one that we could work alongside and was willing to take in all our children.

The three housemothers that were left wanted to go with the children because it was their way of supporting me for what I had gone through for the sake of our children.

It was good that we could work in partnership with others, yet still have the responsibility for our children's school fees, medical needs, food, and provisions.

It meant that someone was on the ground all the time to oversee the care of our children, and this took the pressure off me. It was hard to let go, but I had no choice if I wanted to keep them all together.

Things were going well with Rick Miller, the founder of the orphanage who had taken our children in, and we even met up with him and his wife when they flew into Heathrow on one occasion. He belonged to a Christian organisation based in the USA.

This was, until later in 2014, when the Ebola outbreak happened. Rick and his family were sent back to the States for safety, so Jonathan, a local Sierra Leonean and staff member, was put in charge.

The children under the care of Rick Miller

Jonathan underestimated my knowledge of his country and just saw me as 'a white woman who must have money'!

I insisted he sent spreadsheets so I could see what he wanted, but as time went by a familiar pattern started to emerge. I noticed the cost of items was being greatly inflated, and questioned him. He always had an answer, but little did he realise, so did I!

I looked down his list and saw he was asking for nine dozen schoolbooks for six children, and ten dozen schoolbooks for nine children, twenty-four rulers for eighteen children, and thirty sharpeners! It got worse – sixty pairs of girls' pants and forty-eight pairs of socks!

The final straw was when I saw ninety-two metres of fabric for the girl's school uniforms! Sadly for him, he didn't realise I was once a bridal designer, and therefore I knew exactly how much fabric was needed for our girls' uniforms! And it certainly wasn't ninety-two metres!

The saying "give them an inch and they'll take a yard" had never been so true!

I, of course, reported this to Rick Miller in the States, and the appropriate action was taken, but as the Ebola crisis continued, I felt I had to find other alternatives for the children as things were not satisfactory.

Rick put me in touch with a Christian organisation he knew of called Komeo International Ministries which had recently been formed, and was also based in the USA but working in Freetown.

I felt I had very little choice, as I knew I couldn't go back out.

Putting my faith in Rick, we were put in touch with the organisers of Komeo. This was to be a baptism of fire for me! They were very different and I was really challenged at times. They had already taken in many orphans and were now taking ours as well.

After a while, I became very concerned about their ethics, and on one occasion, I remember them saying that they were really struggling to feed all the children, yet had gone out and bought each of them a Bible!

Whilst this was commendable, I didn't share their views on many things or agree with their financial priorities when it came to the children.

I felt it was more important to buy them much-needed food. After all, if they were hungry, they couldn't exactly eat the Bibles they had been given!

This was something I had never previously come across, but my husband was able to enlighten me as to the customs of folk from the deep south of the USA!

I became more and more concerned. Then, early one morning, our eldest lad Augustine called me. He had run out and gone to his school friend's house to use their phone to call me.

He had heard people at Komeo talking, and all the children were about to be moved somewhere else to join another two hundred children!

I had no knowledge of this and hadn't been informed. I later found out that they couldn't afford the rent and staff for two places.

I also became aware that the children still weren't being fed properly. Even worse, the staff had not been paid for months. I had word that the children were now becoming sick.

By now, it was late 2016 and the Ebola crisis was coming to an end, but still things were not going at all well. I was becoming increasingly concerned about the children's health and welfare.

Chapter 19
Starting All Over Again

I had done everything I could but now I was going to have to consider starting up all over again.

One of the staff, 'Oswald' (not his real name) who was caring for our children wasn't getting paid either. I managed to speak to him and he knew of a house that was up for rent, and big enough for our children.

Over the next few weeks I had to take a huge step of faith and start all over again.

I couldn't leave the children where they were, so with the committee's agreement, we started the process and managed to take our children from where they were, to yet another new home. This was in January 2017.

I had sent money to begin again and buy pots and pans and kitchen equipment, table and chairs and beds for everyone. 'Oswald' brought his wife, who was a nurse, and another housemother to care for our children.

The moving date was the end of February 2017. It was a lot of hard work but I had to do it. They were a family of The Cotton Tree Children!

Whilst all this was going on, I became aware that all was not right with my health and had put off going to see my GP until I had moved the children. They were my priority.

But on March 2nd 2017 I was diagnosed with aggressive stage three breast cancer. Nothing in the world can prepare you for this. It was devastating.

I had to have surgery, followed by radiotherapy. The road to recovery would be long and hard. What on earth was I going to do about the charity?

No matter how I tried, I couldn't manage. Ron and I desperately needed help from the committee.

It had only been in the previous year that committee members felt I should take a step back and allow them to do more, and that I should instead become the charity's ambassador, rather than day-to-day administrator, so here was their chance to step forward. Despite asking, however, no one was able to step up to the plate. Some had jobs and families and couldn't take it on. I desperately needed help more than ever.

With no offers coming forward, I decided to ask one of the committee members who had been a sponsor for a number of years if she would be willing to help out just temporarily until I was well again. She was someone I felt could handle the administration side of things well, and knew most of what had happened over the years. Eventually she agreed. This was good. I felt the charity was in good hands, and that I could concentrate on the long road to recovery.

'Violet' (not her real name) began handling all the emails and I was happy for her to continue. I didn't therefore need to check my emails daily, and neither did Ron.

We just had to concentrate on getting me through this awful time, until one day I happen to catch sight of one of her emails to the rest of the committee saying she felt 'Oswald', our new manager should have his own computer, printer, and office etc. Alarm bells rang, and I had to step in.

'Violet' had no experience or knowledge of life in Sierra Leone, other than what I had told her, and was a career high-flyer.

She knew that when I went out to Freetown, my bedroom was my office.

I had no computer and had to go to the Internet cafe in town, and hope that after two hours in the car to get there, it would be working? This was Africa!

Not only had she offered to help, but she was also in the process of taking over and spending our sponsors' money on many unnecessary items! Of course 'Oswald' (not his real name) would like a new desk, a new computer and a printer! Who wouldn't in Africa! It simply didn't happen.

I had to intervene and point out that we were not in a position financially to buy all these things.

This didn't go down well at all, and certain committee members didn't seem to question her actions either.

'Violet' was a forceful woman which was good in one way, but not in another.

I tried very gently to tell her that this was not how things work in Africa, but I was totally ignored and firmly told she didn't need my help at all. I had to step back as I wasn't strong enough to do anything else.

As time went by, things went from bad to worse, with the committee choosing to go with the decisions 'Violet' was making, a woman they had only heard of and never met, as she lived in Europe.

'Violet' then wrote a letter of resignation saying she couldn't work with such an organisation and that I was using my cancer to get out of my responsibilities!

Nothing could have been further from the truth, but I didn't have the strength I had before to climb back up. So when you hit rock bottom, there isn't anywhere else to go.

Eventually certain other committee members also resigned. I was completely devastated and felt used as a get out for people.

And these were people who claimed to be friends. I had no choice but to step in before 'Violet' parted with a large sum of money.

After she had resigned, 'Violet,' unbeknown to me, had decided to go behind my back and began working with our manager 'Oswald,' who was caring for our children, whilst I was left to pick up the pieces.

She then decided to go out to Freetown to plan her next move with him. 'Violet' was a forceful woman, as I have already said, and determined to get whatever she wanted.

Chapter 20
The Children Are Brainwashed

One day I was sitting, trying to recover from the ordeal I had just been through as a result of cancer and the horrendous situation with the children, when I got an email from someone called Maria Meeks. Maria was a sponsor and I had met her some years before at one of my dancing classes. She was such a lovely person and had been a real support in so many ways.

Her email went something like this… "I'm so sorry to hear of all the problems you've been having and wondered if this may be of help? I have a gardener called Nicholas Sweetland who has gone out to Freetown in Sierra Leone to do voluntary mission work for a year. Would you like me to give you his email address to see if there is anything he could do to help."

Wow! Had I just read that correctly? I re-read it, and my heart began to beat faster with the ring of hope I had just been given.

I sat at my computer in February 2018 and headed the email 'Can you help'. I began to outline the story of what had happened to a man I had never met. I had nothing to lose. A few days later the answer came back, which said, "That is an absolute atrocity of a story! No wonder you got ill! I've just spoken with my friend Pastor David. His immediate response was, 'Yes, of course, we can help her, we share the same vision'! If you knew him like me, you would have a real sense of security, because, believe me, when this guy says he can help, he can!"

I could hardly believe what I was reading! This was simply amazing and an answer to my prayers! And from that day to this, I have never looked back.

Pastor David was coming to the UK in May of 2018 with his wife, so Ron and I went to meet him. It was wonderful. I felt I was back in Sierra Leone as I listened to him talking! He was amazed I could speak Krio and we immediately started a conversation in their language. He quickly realised this 'white woman' knew a thing or two about his homeland and was surprised at the wealth of knowledge and insight I had.

I gave David a special letter I had written to all the children and was to be given to Augustine, our eldest lad, to read to the other children. This was my last hope of telling them how much I loved them, and that I would always be there for them if they ever needed me. I gave them my phone number in the letter, and told them they were to contact me when they were older as their sponsors had left money in our account if and when they wanted to continue their studies at college or university.

Left to right, Nicholas Sweetland, Rosemary Bidwell, David and Threas Keifala

I told David where I thought he could find Augustine, and could do no more.

We had been talking on the phone since February about a way forward for the children. The government had recently issued a statement saying they wanted children like ours to be integrated into family homes, rather than orphanages as it gave them a better home life for their future. Pastor David had contacts with families he knew within his church and approached them to see if they would be willing to take our children. The answer came back with a resounding 'yes'. I would be happy for this, as I knew David would be able to oversee all the children in their different homes and give them the stability they needed for the next stage of their lives.

He and his wife returned home and we began the initial process of David going into their schools to introduce himself to the children and their teachers.

This was short-lived however as we suddenly learnt that 'Violet' had taken all the children without my permission, along with the manager, and moved them to somewhere else she was going to rent.

She even changed the name of the charity, so not only had she taken the children from the stability of their home and school, but they had also lost their identity as 'The Cotton Tree Children'.

The children had all been brain washed and told that I didn't want anything more to do with them and that they didn't want any further contact with me.

I could not believe how anyone could do this to children!

The manager of the home went along with it, as 'Violet' was clearly in charge.

She decided she didn't want to take anything from their Cotton Tree home, so she bought all new furniture! It's hard to imagine what those dear children went through.

I was left utterly devastated. All those years of love and dedication to the children who were now told I had abandoned them.

David was prevented from seeing the children at their schools and could do no more. He was left to tell the families at church what had happened.

He still had my letter to give to the children, so when things had calmed down he set about finding Augustine.

David eventually found him and gave the letter to him. He took it and read it to the children that night. Augustine was their mentor, as he was the eldest.

I had to write to all the children's sponsors, informing them of what had happened.

I had no idea what 'Violet' was planning, so I had to tell the sponsors to cease their money donations. It wasn't just me that had been let down, but the children's sponsors too. Many of them had supported the children since I rescued them in 2007 and 2008 and had become very attached to them.

I assured them that their money would remain in our charity account until the children were older and would be used to further their studies after they left school.

'Violet' managed to 'acquire' the list of sponsors from my list of emails when she was standing in for me, and in June 2018 wrote to each of them, asking for their sponsorship. I heard of this and had to inform the sponsors that I could give no guarantees of where their money would be going.

A while later sponsors received messages from 'Violet' saying, "She had just 'rescued' the children and was only doing it because the kids had asked her to, and would they, their sponsors, like to send a goodbye message"! I was lost for words, and so were the children's sponsors. It seemed we could do nothing more.

Whilst still being brain-washed, Augustine decided to contact me in July 2018 asking me to 'make peace' with 'Violet' and the manager.

I could tell that Augustine had not been given the facts and was torn between believing what 'Violet' had told them and the Grandma Rose who brought him up.

He had been told that I had abandoned him and the others, and that I didn't want anything more to do with them, and this made him angry. He wasn't the Augustine I knew.

It took a long time for him to see that I wasn't the person he was told I was.

He was afraid of me, and feared I would tell 'Violet' he had been in touch. He didn't know if he could trust me.

Then came the news that he, along with two of the other older children, had been moved out, and 'Violet' was taking in more children!

Augustine tried to keep in contact with the other two, but they didn't trust him either, especially when he said he'd been in contact with me. They had been threatened by 'Violet' not to have any contact. 'Violet' was paying for their education, and they knew that if she found out, she would stop their school fees, just as she did with Augustine. As we still had the children's money in our account, it was decided in June 2019 that I should offer an olive branch to 'Violet' and offer to pay for all the children's school fees for the next academic year. Despite what had happened, my interests were still with the children, and I wanted to help them. I knew how expensive things were and thought she might appreciate the offer.

I wrote to 'Violet' offering to pay and had a reply saying,

"The children already have sponsors who will be paying, however we are looking for additional sponsors for the university students, (being the older ones). I have consulted with them about your offer and they have asked me to reiterate their wish to sever all links with you"!

I guess this reminded me of how controlling 'Violet' was.

Little did she realise that Augustine was now in regular contact with me, and he did **not** "wish to sever all links" as she had indicated!

Chapter 21
A Rainbow of Hope

Over the next few months, Augustine learnt to trust me, and seemed better for being away from the home. During this time he began to realise what had happened to him, and could see things differently.

Now that he wanted me to care for him again, I realised that it was time to think about the next stage of his life, as he certainly didn't want anything further to do with 'Violet', and had become very angry with what she had done. He kept asking me to forgive him, as he felt so bad about the things he had said. Of course I forgave him, but there was nothing to forgive really. It showed the deep effects it had had on him.

He began to explain that it was not easy living where he was, as he had to share a room and he couldn't study easily. 'Violet' had also stopped paying his school fees.

In September of 2019 I decided to contact David to see if he could help. He said he had a little room in his compound, which would be perfect for Augustine. He could move in and David would then watch over him as a father figure.

Once again, this was an answer to my prayers. Augustine had been through so much and needed some stability and security.

I managed to get Augustine to go and meet with David to discuss the idea. Augustine was over the moon! The room needed to be cleaned out and already had a bed in it. This was just what Augustine wanted - his own little place where he could start the next phase of his life. After all, he was now twenty-one years old!

He had always been the eldest and was far too old to be with the other children. I had got my Big Chief Augustine back at last! Years before, I had always promised him that when he was seventeen I would get him driving lessons so he could drive our vehicle when I went out, but sadly that wasn't to be.

He became very excited and wanted a little money to buy his bed sheets and a mat to put at his door! It was so lovely to see this young man striding out into adulthood.

He moved in on October 10th 2019. From here he could do his studying and go off to college.

He was now completely free from 'Violet' but did miss the other children.

We now pay for all his education, and David's wife agreed to cook for him too, so he was well looked after. We pay a sum each month towards the upkeep of his little house and his food. I cannot begin to tell you what this has meant!

I sent him some money to buy a cheap phone and a sim card, which cost about forty pounds! This would enable me to have contact with him, and even do video calls on WhatsApp. Something I never thought would ever happen, but it just goes to show, you should never, ever give up hope, and always have patience.

Whilst all this was going on, I had a call from Abi, who by now was living in a room in a shared house, very near to where Pastor David lived, and in the same area where our orphanages had been in Majay Town, Freetown.

She said she was outside one day when a young mother with a month old baby asked if she would hold her baby boy while she went to the toilet. Abi said yes... and she never came back!

Abi was literally left holding the baby!

She set about trying to find her to no avail, so she decided to go to the police and Social Welfare to report the child in case the mother returned. Sadly she never did, so Abi has been bringing up the little boy as her own. She initially named him Mohammed, as her friend had a little boy with that name, but in time she asked Pastor David if he would baptise him, to which he agreed. It was then that she spoke to me about his name and asked my husband and I to choose a name, as she wasn't sure about her choice of Mohammed. We had a think and decided we'd like to call him Luke, so on September 1st 2018 he was duly baptised Luke Mohammed!

Abi and Rosie with little Luke and Luke Mohammed Solomon at his christening, 2019

By now it was getting a little crowed in Abi's single room with Rosie, Abi's daughter who was now fourteen years old, so she asked her friend if Rosie could go and live with her, and she agreed. This wasn't ideal but life in Sierra Leone is very different and children become very resilient to change. Their main focus is their education. This is their only hope of getting out of the situation they sadly find themselves in.

It was hard for Abi, and for a long time, she didn't want to tell me, as she felt I would think ill of her. Rosie used to visit her mum and baby Luke at weekends, but it meant a long journey across town of a few hours.

Since I adopted Abi when she had Rosie at the age of fourteen, I have personally been paying for Rosie's education, just as I paid for all Abi's.

Then in Christmas 2019, she went to stay with Abi and also visited Pastor David and his family. She loved it there, as it was such a loving family home. She even ended up staying over with them some nights.

David and Theresa are a wonderful couple with big Christian hearts, and had already taken in two orphan boys, as well as a lovely teenage girl called Ruthlynn who was the same age as Rosie. Rosie would share the same room as Ruthlynn when she went to visit. They were also given a little baby girl to care for, who they called Davida! No wonder Rosie loved being there!

Rosie going to school in 2019

Rosie posing in her native country, 2020

All was going well until I received a message from the Cotton Tree children saying they needed my help! This came as a complete surprise, as I hadn't had any contact with them for a very long time. Why would they want my help?

I also had a text message from the manager saying the children sent their love! After a strong cup of coffee, I decided to text the manager to see if everything was ok

What came back left me speechless. 'Violet' had left the children and walked away.

She had also cancelled all their sponsors! What on earth had happened to make her do this?

Apparently she wanted the manager to sign a contract document regarding the children and he refused, so she went to get the police and demanded they open the gates of the compound. The police refused, as their priority was the welfare of the children. 'Violet' objected in a fit of rage and left.

I was asked by the manager for my advice as 'Violet' was still using all the children's photos on her new social media charity page. The manager was far from happy with this, as 'Violet' appeared to be using the children's pictures to assist with gaining more sponsorship.

I strongly advised the manager and his board to re-name the orphanage as soon as possible and disassociate himself with 'Violet'. They came up with several new names and asked me to choose one, which I did. They also wanted me to be on the board, but I preferred to remain as an advisor. We are now supporting the children once again, and for the first time since 2014 I am receiving regular updates of the children and lovely photos of them all!

Who would ever have thought it!? Certainly not me!

My lovely children once again in 2020

Chapter 22
I Have a Dream

You may recall me saying that Rosie was enjoying visiting Pastor David at Christmas. Unfortunately Abi's friend, who was looking after her, was no longer able to do this, so Rosie needed a new home.

It transpired that Rosie had also been staying with David and Theresa at weekends after Christmas and really loved living there!

Once again Pastor David came to the rescue, and after a few discussions we agreed that Rosie would go and live with them and their family.

We moved her few possessions over and she now goes to a better school and is nearer to Abi and Luke. She also has Augustine living in the compound, so it couldn't be better!

I never thought this wonderful story would end so happily! Did you?

My 'Big Chief Augustine' and Rosie in 2020

One day, whilst writing this book, I was sitting outside having a cup of tea in the garden, when I saw an ant pulling a dead bee across the patio. I watched as it worked tirelessly to drag this bee across the slabs to where he wanted it to go.

Every so often the ant would stop, presumably to rest, but it never gave up.

It's hard to believe that something so small would be prepared to take on the challenge of something so much bigger than itself?

This reminded me a bit of what I was doing when I was working in Sierra Leone.

I was one small, insignificant person who was prepared to work tirelessly, just like the ant, to achieve my goal.

I remember when I was first thinking of going out to Sierra Leone I attended a seminar by the charity I initially went out to Africa with.

The person was speaking about 'the power of one' and what a difference that can make.

Through the power of 'one person', I was able to achieve what I thought was the impossible!

I always felt that if I could make a difference to just one person in my lifetime, then my life would have been worthwhile. I have now made a life-changing difference to many children living in a Third World country where they had no hope and no future, and some would not have survived if I hadn't been like the ant and taken on something much larger than myself.

As a Christian, I also know how all this has been possible, through my faith and my belief in the power of ONE!

I'd like to finish with a little story that you might like to think about.

One day a young boy was walking along a beach when he saw hundreds of starfish that had been washed up on the shore. He went up to where they were, and one by one he started to throw them back into the sea.

A man was following the young boy and saw what he was doing. He was puzzled, and as he got closer he said to the boy "Why are you spending all this time throwing those starfish back in the water. It's a waste of your time, you'll never do it as there are hundreds".

The young boy looked up at the man, and picked up one of the starfish. He then very purposefully threw it into the water, and looking back at the man said,

"Well, it's made a difference to that one!"

We can all make a difference to this world we live in.

I have a dream… to one day go back one last time to see the wonderful children of The Cotton Tree Children's Trust.

The End

Appendix
In Their Own Words

<u>Written by Augustine Conteh in 2020</u>

My name is Augustine Conteh and I am 22 years old. I am now planning to enter my public exam, commonly known as the West African Senior Secondary School Certificate Examination. W.A.S.S.C.E.

My father died of a urinary tract infection in June 2006 when I was seven years old. I also lost my mother as she died of breast cancer.

On the 13th July 2006 a sad status in our country as orphan numbers mounted higher. Tears of bitterness started running down my eyes. Thoughts started fighting within me, who else can take the place of my dearly loved mother in this wicked world?

Thank God among the relatives, God touched the heart of one of my uncles by the name of John Conteh who expressed an interest in helping me, but he too was not financially strong enough for my upkeep.

One day a friend of his came to visit him and explained there was a charity being run by a white woman who was assisting children of our type. Just after his friend's directions, my uncle made a swift move to the place where he found Grandma Rose. According to him, he was requested to bring all relevant documents about me to Social Welfare in 2007.

June 16th is African Children's day and was also the day in 2007 that I entered the orphanage home.

My Uncle and I arrived at the Social Welfare office where I found five other kids waiting for the processing of their documents. On that very day we were seven in number marked as the second batch to be registered for the home on completion of the registration process. Seven of us got into a vehicle that took us to our new home (an orphanage) at Morgan Lane, Marjay Town where we found the first batch of kids, Rose-Mary Soloman or Rosie Posey as we call her being one of them.

I can still remember when Alimamy was crying all night long.

Actually it was not easy for us, but thank God the aunties or housemothers were so kind and lovely to us.

In 2008, another batch of eight kids were brought into the orphanage.

A sad moment came back into our lives five years on when we came to realise that we had to move into our second home just up the road. We loved our home but we needed more room and Grandma Rose wanted to live with us on her visits.

We were only there three years when Grandma Rose was taken from us suddenly and sent back to England. We were so discouraged with such misfortunes.

After our displacement from Marjay Town we landed at Waterloo at an orphanage called Children Redemption run by Pastor Rick Miller. We were only there a few months before Ebola struck our Country.

We were then all informed to get ready to move once again to Wellington, to another orphanage. We all started crying bitterly for someone to rescue us from such agony.

On 12th June 2015, the poor orphan kids were packed into a vehicle and sent to the Wellington Orphanage. It was there that we met with a man named 'Oswald' (not his real name). We remained there until January 5th 2017 when we were moved yet again to another much bigger orphanage which was supported by Komeo which housed some two hundred kids. We only got fed twice a day and became unwell.

Grandma Rose heard of this and wanted us Cotton Tree kids to live in a smaller house as we did before so in early March of 2017 all the kids were moved into a new home with 'Oswald' as the manager.

Our new home was located in Waterloo and just after we had moved, we came to realise that our beloved Grandma Rose, the director of The Cotton Tree Trust had been diagnosed with cancer. All the kids were very worried about her and we were all very sad. 'Oswald' called a meeting with staff and kids. He asked everyone to give their opinion about Grandma, but everyone refused to contribute. We were told that another person had been put in charge of administration until Grandma had recovered. 'Oswald' was now in touch with a woman called 'Violet' (not her real name) who called concerning the issue of running the home.

In 2018 things became very tedious for the kids and staff. 'Oswald' was unable to bear the situation because he claimed he was not getting any support from Grandma Rose, which was untrue.

'Violet' gave him her answers and they had a meeting. They decided to work together without Grandma knowing and 'Violet' assured 'Oswald' he would have everything he wanted. She even came out to Sierra Leone to meet with 'Oswald' and put on a big party for all the kids and told us we were no longer Cotton Tree children as she had changed the name of the charity and was moving us all to another place. We were told to leave everything behind as 'Violet' was going to buy all new furniture and bedding. It was really heartrending after all of Grandma's efforts.

'Violet' sent some money to do all the administrative work for changing the name of the orphanage. The kids didn't have any choices because everything was done under the control of 'Violet' and 'Oswald'.

Then one day in 2019 'Violet' and her husband visited Sierra Leone and saw the document compiled by Social Welfare and were not pleased. The reason was that most of the documents were signed by 'Oswald' stating that he was the founder and manager of the new home. 'Violet' and her husband tried to get 'Oswald' to sign the document saying she was 'the new founder' and 'Oswald' refused. 'Violet' got very angry and asked me and another boy to go with her to the police station to get them to come to the home and meet with 'Oswald".

I didn't like her attitude at all. They were arguing about who was the founder, instead of concentrating on the best interests of us children. Grandma Rose always put the children's needs first in everything she did for us.

'Violet' and her husband left very cross because she couldn't have her own way.

Later in 2019 'Violet' and her husband returned to Sierra Leone, but they didn't go to visit the kids once. Instead they chose to give money to some young men they met on the beach where they were staying in a very expensive hotel.

They had turned their backs on all the kids they had taken from Grandma Rose and even cancelled all their sponsors, including the child they had been sponsoring for many years and called their daughter, giving her false hope, so now the kids had nothing. I feel angry because she has used the sponsors' money for something else when she should have been caring for our kids.

All the kids had been fed untruths about our beloved Grandma Rose. We were told she had turned her back on us and wasn't supporting us anymore. Now after all this time I know the truth. Grandma Rose would never abandon us. She loves us too much.

I just want to take this opportunity to say a big thank you to Grandma Rose for all her relentless effort and labour for looking after me. She has really been a huge blessing in my life.

Grandma Rose and Papa Ron have also taken up the challenge for my feeding and that of my accommodation. They also help me by paying for all my schooling and send me a little pocket money each month.

I am very blessed to have them as my loving and caring parents. They really mean the world to me. May God continue to prolong their days.

From your Big Chief Augustine.

Written by 'Rosie Posey' in 2020

My name is Rose Mary Solomon, or Rosie Posey as Grandma Rose calls me. I am the daughter of Abibatu Solomon. The young girl Grandma Rose adopted years ago.

I was born on 2nd April 2004, that is what is on my birth certificate but Grandma says I was actually born in September 2004, but my mother could not remember the date when she registered me!

Grandma Rose took me and my mother to London in 2006 to make us better so we could have a better life when we returned to our homeland.

When I came back to Sierra Leone, I was told that Grandma Rose had opened an orphanage. I was still a little girl and was in the orphanage with other children where we grew up together until one bad day when things were falling apart.

Grandma Rose was taken sick and we did not see her. I felt all alone but I have family and friends and love once again around me.

My friends at school were giving me courage because some had lost a parent and I had Grandma as my parent because I don't know my father, so I have courage.

Grandma always gave me a present when my birthday came, and in the holidays when she came, she took us all to the beach to have fun.

My mum's aunty was called aunty Vero. She took me to stay there but aunty Vero's grandson didn't like me. He always made fun of me that I was an orphan because I was staying in the orphanage.

When I went to primary four I was almost driven from the school because of aunty Vero's behaviour. She did not pay my school fees and because of that my mother took me to another place. I went to stay with a woman called aunty Janet. She was a good woman but she liked money. The little money that my mother was having she gave to her for me to go to school. When I was with aunty Janet I sat my NPSC exam and I went to secondary school.

I was in DSS 2 when my mother called and told me that Grandma Rose wanted to speak with me. I was so happy as I thought she would come and take me away so that I would be a good person in future and I would take care of Grandma and my mother. I was happy to hear Grandma's voice that day.

I went back to stay with my mother till DSS 3 and she took me to my uncle Sheku's house. I was with uncle Sheku when I went to senior school.

I knew Pastor David and his family and they were the reason uncle Sheku drove me out of his house because I always came to see my mother at weekends so that we could talk. Since I came to live with Pastor David and his family in 2020, I am so happy and he took me as his daughter and I still have my beloved Grandma Rose as she gives me all that I want in life and she even make way for me so that I could have a holiday in England and spend holiday time with her and my Grandpa, but the coronavirus hit England and Pastor David and me could not visit.

Thank you Grandma and thank you Grandpa. May God bless you because you are my grandparents. I love you Grandma. I love you Grandpa xxxx

Written by Alan Daley

I met Rosie Bidwell at a dance lesson one night and she explained that she had set up an orphanage in Sierra Leone, so a group of us met afterwards for a chat and I was able to find out all about the orphanage Rosie had set up.

I had been looking for a charity to support and as a child had supported a missionary family in Chad so had a connection with Africa from an early age. After hearing Rosie's story, I decided to get involved with the charity.

Around one Christmas time I had the opportunity at short notice to accompany Rosie to the orphanage in Sierra Leone. Rosie had prepared me for what was to come, and she had prepared me well, as my expectations were not very high as we approached the orphanage in Freetown after a torturous journey over land air and sea.

When we finally arrived at the orphanage, and the children were wonderful and happy as they came to greet us, they were well cared for by the aunties who cared for them at the orphanage. It was a wonderful experience and a feeling of great worth being able to not only see the children in person but be involved in their lives, helping them both practically and emotionally.

These children had no future or hope but now they were well fed, given a home to live in and had been provided with an education and a bright future in a country that had little to offer.

The living conditions were not what you would expect in England, but they had a bed to sleep in, a school that they could attend and food to eat every day.

I had already been given two sisters to adopt financially when I first committed to support the charity, and to meet them face to face was very moving and special. We were walking to collect water one day when Ishatu, one of the sisters, held my hand and said "Can we call you Daddy", this was a very special moment and made the bond even stronger. To this day many years later she still calls me Daddy and keeps in touch when she can by phone.

On the occasions I have been able to visit the orphanage I had a feeling of happiness and worth being able to be a part of the lives of these small children once without any future or any hope in life, to now be able to be a valuable asset to Sierra Leone.

I have visited Sierra Leone on a further occasion and as the children got older it was wonderful to see how the lives of these orphans had changed and had been given an opportunity in life that they would never have had if Rosie had not been given the vision to start the charity.

Although there had been many challenges and difficulties over the years, Rosie has been true to all the children and never given up on them. Many of them would probably not have survived if Rosie had not given them a future and a hope. And I am glad that I have been given the opportunity to make a small contribution to the lives of these children.

Written by Nicholas Sweetland

My own experience of Sierra Leone was crazy!

I had a very definite calling to go to Freetown, in Sierra Leone that took me by surprise and meant having the courage to quit my gardening business to go and live there for a while. I knew pastor David who lived there, through my church and arranged to live next door to him in a hut, living a very simple life as one of the locals.

It was while I was there that one of my gardening customers contacted me and asked if I'd like to talk to a friend of hers who had also been to Sierra Leone and needed help with her orphan children.

It's been said that I have a way of 'opening doors' and this was one of those occasions. I was just in the right place at the right time to hear Rosemary's amazing story and introduce her to my friend Pastor David Keifala. He had a particular passion for helping vulnerable children in his country and when I told him about Rosemary's situation, he was only too happy to see if he could help.

The work over there is still always in need of ongoing funding and carrying on the incredible work Rosemary started. The children that have been rescued will be the next generation of leaders over there. And it'll be the love that they have received, that they will pass on to others in their own time, permeating their country more and more with the goodness of warm hearts and the influence of golden people like Grandma Rose!

Written by Ron Toft

It took me only a few weeks after first meeting Rosie in May 2014 to realise what a very special lady she was – and still is!

Throughout her life, Rosie has always put other people first and possessed a kind, caring, loving nature. That's why, I guess, she used to be a nurse (only having to give up that career because of a bad back), a foster mum to many severely mentally and/or physically disabled children and shutting down her highly successful bridal-wear business in Warwick to set up an orphanage for street children in Sierra Leone. Her magnetic personality, her ability to captivate, charm and enthuse people when telling them about her Sierra Leone 'adventure' and persuading them to donate money to her charity or sponsor one or more Cotton Tree children, has been a revelation to me. Rosie is a truly remarkable woman – one in a million. Hardly surprising, therefore, I fell in love with her and persuaded her to marry me!"

I hope you have enjoyed reading my book.

If you feel inspired to make a donation or wish to know more, please contact me.

Rosemary Bidwell

Email: cottontreechild@gmail.com

Thank you on behalf of all our children.